237

ID0998369

Our modern world is dependent on the engines that put power, or energy, to work for us. Earlier people had only muscle power, wind power, and water power. Today we use many additional kinds of power to run our cars and trains, our ships and planes and rockets, our vacuum cleaners and washing machines, our television receivers and other electronic devices.

In this book, Sam and Beryl Epstein give a lucid account of man's continuing search for new and more efficient methods for producing power. Joseph and Eva Cellini contribute expert drawings and explanatory diagrams. Together, text and illustrations explain the workings of gasoline and Diesel engines, turbines and steam engines, rockets and jets, electric generators and nuclear reactors.

All About Engines and Power *is a stimulating introduction to a subject of widespread interest.*

621.4
Ep85a

All About Engines and Power

31097

All About

Illustrated by Joseph & Eva Cellini

allabout
books

Sam_{uel} & Beryl Epstein

Engines and Power

This special edition is printed and distributed by
arrangement with the originators and publishers of
Allabout Books, RANDOM HOUSE, Inc., New York, by

E. M. HALE AND COMPANY
EAU CLAIRE, WISCONSIN

The Library
Special Childrens Collection
WITHDRAWN
Saint Francis College
Fort Wayne, Indiana

For helpful suggestions about this book, grateful acknowledgment is made to Ira M. Freeman, professor of physics, Rutgers University; J. J. Jaklitsch, Jr., editor of *Mechanical Engineering* (American Society of Mechanical Engineers); and G. C. Baxter Rowe, associate editor of *Electrical Engineering* (American Institute of Electrical Engineers).

© Copyright, 1962, by Sam and Beryl Epstein

All rights reserved under International and Pan-American Copyright Conventions. Published in New York by Random House, Inc., and simultaneously in Toronto, Canada, by Random House of Canada, Limited.

Library of Congress Catalog Card Number: 62–9007
Manufactured in the United States of America

Design by GUY FLEMING

Contents

All About Engines and Power

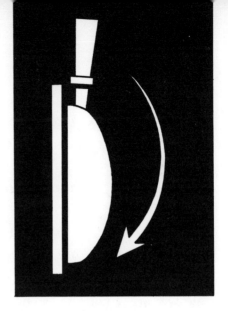

1

Power in Our Lives

DID YOU EVER THINK how much work is done when we simply push a button, move a lever, turn a dial, snap a switch, or step on a pedal?

A printer pushes a button. A block-long machine begins to print newspapers at the rate of thousands an hour.

A crane operator moves a lever. A 20-ton load is picked up from one place and set down in another.

A scientist presses buttons. A computing machine solves a complicated mathematical problem within a few seconds.

A missile expert pulls a switch. A giant rocket takes off on a journey into space.

A housewife turns a dial. A machine washes her family's laundry.

You push a button or turn a dial—and entertainment comes to you over many miles through a radio or a television set. You push another button or snap a switch —and a room is warmed or cooled or flooded with light.

We depend so much on push buttons that people often say we are living in a push-button age.

In fact, we depend so much on all our buttons, levers, dials, switches, and pedals that we sometimes forget that those devices do not really do any work at all.

Those devices are only controls, rather like traffic policemen controlling the flow of traffic, and ordering it to go or stop.

When you want a job done, and push a button to start a machine, you are really giving the go signal to a flow of power—or, as a scientist would say, to a flow of energy. That power runs the engine, or machine, that does the work.

In lands where there is a great deal of power, and many engines, a great deal of work gets done. The United States uses nearly half of all the power produced in the entire world. That is why Americans can have more things than most other people have.

Only when plenty of power is produced everywhere

can all people have what they need and want for a good life—plenty of food, pure water, clothes, houses, schools, books, medicine, electric lights, automobiles, and hundreds of other things.

Early man used muscle power—his own and that of animals.

2

Muscles, Water, and Wind

THOUSANDS OF YEARS AGO, prehistoric man had neither engines nor the power to run them. He had only muscle power.

He used his own muscle power for hunting and gathering food, and for protecting himself from his enemies. The man with the strongest muscles was usually the leader of his group or tribe.

Then man learned to make use of the muscle power of animals.

He tamed the wild dog. He taught the animal to

help him hunt, and to protect him from attack.

He tamed the wild ox, the elephant, and other very strong animals. He taught them to carry his burdens and turn his heavy millstones.

Sometimes animals also operated the earliest irrigation engines. Those engines were big wheels with buckets attached to the rim. As the wheels turned, the buckets dipped water up out of a stream and dumped it into a trough.

But prehistoric man also discovered that there were two other kinds of power he could use. Both were free for him to take. They were the power of moving water and the power of the wind.

The Power of Moving Water

MAN PROBABLY DISCOVERED the power of moving water by watching branches and tree trunks float down a river. Then he learned to sit astride a floating tree trunk, and let himself be carried downstream. When he did that, he was using water power to take himself from one place to another. After a while he built rafts and other craft to make better use of this kind of power.

The people of the Middle East, in the lands along the Nile and the Red Sea, may have been the first to use the power of moving water in another way. They attached paddles to a bucket-rimmed water wheel. They let the flowing stream push against the paddles and turn

In the past, water wheels were one of the few sources of power.

the wheel around. The turning wheel lifted water from a river to the planted fields on the river's bank without the use of any muscle power at all.

When men learned how to attach a water-driven wheel to a millstone, they could use water power to grind their grain.

As time went by, men learned how to attach a water-driven wheel to other devices too. These could do many kinds of work with the help of water power.

By the middle of the thirteenth century, Germans were installing water wheels in the Rhine River, and using water power to operate the big bellows on the furnaces of ironworks.

By the middle of the fourteenth century, men were using water-powered saws to cut logs into beams and flat boards.

The Power of Wind

THE POWER OF WIND—that is, the power of moving air—was probably also discovered by accident, many thousands of years ago. It proved very useful for carrying men across a lake in which there was no current powerful enough to push a raft. Men held up primitive sails, made of woven mats or animal skins, and let the wind push against those sails.

When they learned how to set their sails at an angle to the wind, and steer a zigzag course, they could use

wind power even when the wind was not blowing in the direction they wanted to go. Until the last century, most ships were driven by wind power.

Men also fastened big blades or sails to a wheel. This gave them a windmill. It could be used in the same way a water-powered wheel was used. It could be made to do many kinds of work.

From the twelfth century on, windmills were used widely in Europe. The whole coast of Holland was changed when men discovered that windmills could be used to pump water. The Dutch walled off large areas of seacoast marshes, built high earth dikes around them, and then pumped the water out of the marshes with the help of windmills. In that way Holland gained thousands of acres of rich new farmland.

3

The Need for More Power

BY THE TIME the first settlers came to America, wind and water power were being used in many ways. Some American pioneers used one, some used another, depending on where they settled.

The swift streams of hilly New England provided the power for many water wheels. New Englanders used water power to saw wood, grind grain, make gunpowder, and pump air into the furnaces of iron forges.

The flat fields of Long Island, where there were no swift-flowing streams, became dotted with windmills.

Usually, if a settler lived near a stream, he preferred a water wheel to one driven by the wind. A windmill might stand useless for many days if no wind was blowing. Water was more dependable. Of course a stream might dry up in the summer. But a man knew when that was likely to happen, and could plan his work accordingly. Or he might dam the stream, storing up enough water to turn his wheel even in a dry season.

In the meantime, while the first American colonies were being settled, great changes were taking place in Europe. The population was growing. More and more farmers were moving to the cities, where they could no longer weave their own cloth or grow their own food. New businesses had to be started to supply their needs. There was a greater need for such metals as tin and iron. The demand for coal for fuel rose too. New mines were opened, and old mines were dug deeper and deeper into the earth.

In those days mines were operated entirely by muscle power. Human muscle power dug the ore or coal out of the ground. Animal muscle power worked the hoists that hauled it to the surface. In England, some of the mine shafts went down so far that underground water seeped into them. In those mines, animal muscle power hauled the dangerous seepage out of the mines in huge buckets.

But as time went by, more and more water seeped into some of the very deep mines. Finally the mine owners could not keep them dry, even when they had dozens of horses or oxen hauling up water twenty-four hours a day. Men couldn't work in those flooded shafts. Mines had to be closed down. Mine owners grew very worried. They sought the help of mechanics and inventors. "Find a way to pump our mines dry, and keep them dry," urged the mine owners.

Water pumps had been invented long before. The problem was to find some kind of power which could operate a large pump day in and day out, deep at the bottom of a mine shaft. Wind power could operate a pump—but wind power wasn't dependable enough. Water power could operate a pump too—but few mines were close beside swiftly flowing streams.

The power which finally solved the miners' problem was also the first important step toward our modern mechanized civilization. It was the power of steam. Men didn't discover this new kind of power by accident. They found it instead by hard work, by studying what earlier scientists had learned, and by adding to that knowledge certain new ideas of their own.

The Steam Engine

WHEN INVENTORS BEGAN to search for a solution to the problem of the flooded mines, in the early 1600's, they didn't immediately think of steam as a useful source of power. The first engines they built, using steam, are sometimes called steam engines. Those machines should really be called *atmospheric engines* instead, because they made use of the weight of the atmosphere that presses down on the earth's surface.

Atmospheric Pressure

THE EARTH'S ATMOSPHERE, or air, is like an invisible blanket several hundred miles thick, completely surrounding the globe. This air blanket is not equally "heavy," or dense, all the way through. At the earth's surface it is denser than it is at the top of the blanket. This is because the air at the surface of the earth is being squeezed down by the weight of all the air above it.

Air isn't a heavy substance. But there is so much of it pressing down on the earth that its total weight is tremendous. A single foot of the earth's surface supports over a ton of atmosphere. A single square inch of the earth's surface supports about 15 pounds of atmosphere.

Every square inch of the surface of your body bears this same 15-pound weight or pressure. Why doesn't that pressure squash you flat? Because every hollow inside your body is also filled with air. The pressure of the air inside your body exactly equals the pressure of the air outside. The two pressures are therefore balanced. That's why you do not feel either one.

Everyone make use of the weight of the atmosphere —that is, of atmospheric pressure. You use it when you drink milk or some other liquid through a straw.

Put a straw into a glass of milk. You will see that

the milk rises up inside the straw until it reaches a level just about equal to the level of the milk in the glass itself. This happens because the atmospheric pressure is not pressing down any harder on the milk-inside-the-straw than on the milk-inside-the-glass. Therefore the milk-inside-the-straw rises up to the same level as the rest of the liquid.

But if you suck on the straw, you remove some of the air inside it. Then there will be less pressure inside the straw than outside. The two pressures become un-balanced. As soon as this happens, the greater pressure—the pressure pushing down on the milk-in-the-glass—forces more milk into the bottom of the straw, and pushes it upward.

You may think you are "sucking" the milk upward. Actually you took air out of the straw, leaving some room inside it. And the atmospheric pressure, trying to fill that space, pushed more milk up into the straw until it reached your mouth.

A water pump mounted on a pipe at the top of an ordinary well operates on this same principle. This kind of pump has two main parts. One is the *cylinder*, a tube with an opening at the bottom that can be closed by a valve, like a trap door. The other is the *piston*, a sort of plug that fits snugly inside the cylinder and can slide up and down in it. A hole runs through the piston, and this too can be opened or shut by a valve.

When the piston moves from the bottom of the cylinder to the top, its valve shuts tightly. The piston pushes out ahead of itself some of the air that is inside the cylinder. This reduces the pressure inside the cylinder, below the piston, just as you reduce the pressure inside a drinking straw when you suck on it. And in this case, too, the pressure inside the cylinder becomes less than the pressure outside. So the greater outside pressure, pushing down on the water in the well, forces some of that water up the pipe and into the cylinder.

When the piston returns to the bottom of the cylinder, the piston's valve opens. This allows the water in the lower part of the cylinder to pass through the piston's hole into the upper part of the cylinder. Then the piston moves upward a second time, with its valve again shut,

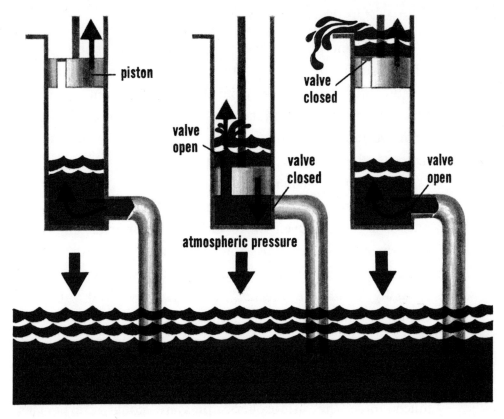

A lift pump uses atmospheric pressure to raise water.

and pushes the water ahead of it and out of the cylinder.

As the piston moves upward that second time, of course, it again leaves a low-pressure space behind it. And that space is once more filled with water. Therefore when the piston of a pump is moved up and down repeatedly, it lifts water out of the cylinder with each stroke. At the same time each stroke permits atmospheric pressure to refill the cylinder from the well.

A vacuum cleaner has an electric fan, or air pump, which takes air out of the cleaner. This reduces the air pressure inside. Air from the outside then rushes in through the hose to make the two pressures equal again. That rushing air carries with it dust and crumbs and deposits them in the cleaner bag.

The word *vacuum* means a perfectly empty space. But it is not possible to empty every particle of air out of a space, even with the most powerful air pump ever made. No matter how long and hard the pump works, there is always some air left. So every vacuum is really a *partial vacuum.* When engineers talk about a vacuum, that is what they mean.

Men were talking a great deal about vacuums in the early 1600's, when they were trying to solve the problem of the flooded mines. They had already discovered how much force the atmospheric pressure could exert. They were trying to think of some way to put that force to work. But they also knew that atmospheric pressure can do work only where there is a vacuum. So they were trying to find the best way to create a vacuum at a flooded mine without using muscle power.

The Somerset Pump

FINALLY AN ENGLISH NOBLEMAN figured out a method for creating a vacuum with the aid of steam. He was Edward Somerset, the Marquess of Worcester.

Somerset spent several years as a prisoner in the Tower of London. While he was in prison he wrote a book which described his invention. It was published in 1663.

Somerset knew that a few drops of water, brought to a boil, produce a great amount of steam. He knew that the opposite of that fact is also true. A lot of steam produces only a few drops of liquid when it is *condensed*—that is, when it is cooled down and turned back into water again. Steam, in fact, takes up about 2,000 times as much space as the water from which it comes.

Somerset therefore tried an experiment. He filled a cylinder with steam, sealed it tightly, and then let the steam condense. He reasoned that the only thing inside the cooled cylinder would be a few drops of water. The cylinder would be almost empty.

The experiment worked. A partial vacuum was formed in the cold cylinder.

Somerset next built a pump for the well that supplied water to his castle. The pump used steam to create a vacuum in its cylinder. The pump operator first filled the cylinder with steam from a boiler. As the steam condensed, forming a vacuum, water from the well was pushed up into the cylinder. Then, by means of valves, the operator allowed more steam to enter the cylinder. The new batch of steam pushed the water out through a pipe leading to a high tank. The steam was doing much the same thing a water-pump piston does. It was causing the cylinder to be filled with water, and then pushing the water out.

Somerset had succeeded in making a machine that pumped water without using muscle power, wind power, or water power. But even an improved model of the engine he invented didn't solve the problem of the flooded mines. It simply wasn't practical for that purpose.

For one thing, the engine had to be quite close to

Somerset used steam to create a vacuum in the cylinder of his pump.

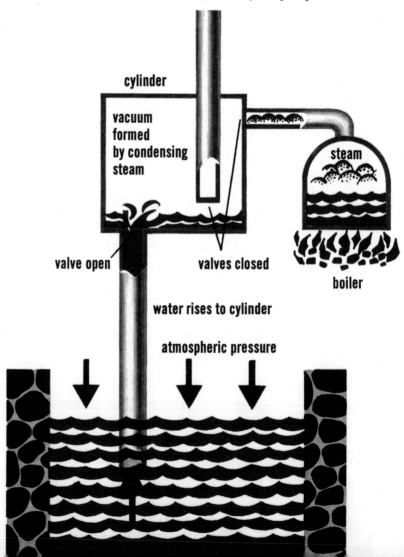

the water it was pumping. That meant that the engine would have to be installed right at the bottom of a mine, where the water seepage occurred. And if the pump failed, and the mine was flooded again, the engine would be flooded too, and ruined.

What the mine owners needed was an engine that could be installed at the top of a mine. There it would be safe, and there it could easily be repaired if it failed to work.

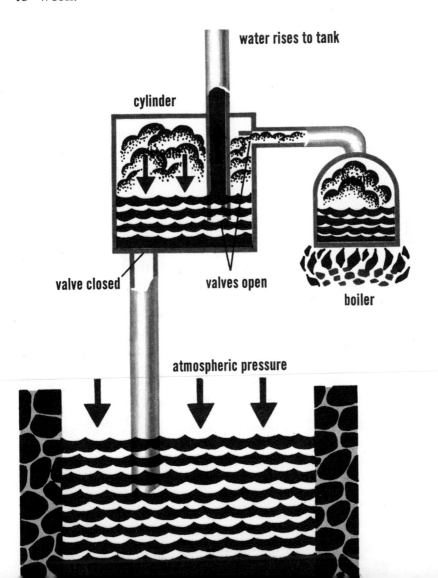

The Newcomen Engine

ONE OF THE MEN who learned about Somerset's pump was a hardware merchant, Thomas Newcomen, born in the English town of Dartmouth four years before Somerset died. And it was Thomas Newcomen, with the help of his friends, who succeeded in making the kind of engine the mine owners needed.

Newcomen's device was also an atmospheric engine that used steam to make a vacuum. But Newcomen didn't use the vacuum to lift up water directly. Instead he used the vacuum in his cylinder to move a piston. And the piston, by means of a long rod, operated a water pump installed at the very bottom of a mine.

To speed up the action of his engine, Newcomen installed a water sprinkler in the cylinder. As soon as the cylinder filled with steam, the sprinkler sprayed cold water into it. This cold water chilled the steam and condensed it almost instantly.

Newcomen's first engines were controlled entirely by hand. A man or boy opened each valve in turn. First he opened the steam valve. Next he opened the water-sprinkler valve. Then he opened a drain valve that let the water inside the cylinder run off. Then he started the process all over again. The engine could operate only as quickly as its operator could open and close the various valves.

Newcomen's engine, placed at the top of a mine shaft, could operate a pump at the bottom.

rocker arm

cold-water
tank

piston

cylinder

team valve

cold-water
valve

valve
control
rod

rod to pump
in mine

steam boiler

Finally someone—certain stories say it was a "valve boy" named Humphrey Potter in 1713—decided that the engine could be made to operate its own valves. He tied strings to the valve handles, and attached the strings to various moving parts of the engine. When the piston was pushed down by atmospheric pressure, its movement pulled the strings that opened first the draining valve and next the steam valve. When the piston moved to the top of the steam-filled cylinder, its motion pulled other strings. And those strings shut off the steam valve and opened the water-sprinkling valve that condensed the steam.

Engine builders quickly realized that automatic valve control speeded up the engine's operation. Soon most Newcomen engines had a system of control rods to operate the valves. Rods were more dependable than strings.

Newcomen's engines also became larger, as time went on. Some had pistons six feet across, moving as much as eight feet up and down in their cylinders. Such engines did a remarkable job in helping to save England's mines.

Every Newcomen engine, however, had one serious drawback. It wasted a lot of the steam that was fed into its cylinder. This meant that it wasted a lot of the coal that had to be burned to heat the water that produced the steam. Mine owners were now worried over the amount of coal they had to use to keep their mines dry.

Newcomen knew why his engine was so wasteful—or, as engineers say, so *inefficient*. He knew that each jet of cold water, sprayed into the cylinder to condense the steam, also cooled the cylinder. This meant that the next charge of steam poured into a cold cylinder and condensed immediately against the chilly walls. The fresh steam continued to condense until its own heat had finally reheated the cylinder. Then the cylinder could finally fill with hot steam again, and produce the piston's next downward stroke. It was the cold cylinder that wasted so much steam.

But Newcomen didn't know how to cool and condense steam without also cooling the cylinder. Neither did the many engineers who built and installed Newcomen engines. The man who solved the problem at last was a Scotsman named James Watt.

James Watt, Mechanic

JAMES WATT LIVED in Glasgow. As a young man he earned his living by making and repairing laboratory instruments for the University of Glasgow.

One day in 1763 Watt was asked to repair the model of a Newcomen engine. He knew very little about such things. But he was an expert mechanic, and he was soon able to put the little model in working order. He was watching it in operation, on his workbench, when he decided it used a great deal of steam for so small a machine. He made some careful tests. Soon he proved that only one-fourth of all the steam it used could be turned into useful work.

At that moment Watt joined the dozens of other men who were trying to solve the problem of the chilled cylinder.

The solution finally came to him, after weeks of work, when he was taking a walk one fine Sunday.

"Why not," he asked himself, "let the steam from the cylinder run into a tank, when it is time for the steam to be condensed back into water? The tank can be kept cold all the time, for quick condensing. But the cylinder itself will never get cold, because no cold water will ever be shot into it. Then, when the cylinder fills with steam again, the steam will stay hot and will not be wasted."

Watt went to work immediately to put his new idea into practice. He built a small experimental model of a Newcomen atmospheric engine, and added to it his *condensing tank*, as it is called.

He had to overcome many difficulties. Almost fifteen years of hard work went by before Watt was ready to install a big working model of his new engine at the head of a mine. It was very successful. Because the cylinder didn't have to be reheated all the time, the engine worked much faster than the old Newcomen engine. And it was much cheaper to operate too, because it didn't waste so much steam.

By then—the year was 1777—Watt had two new

ideas he wanted to try out. One idea had come to him when he saw how swiftly the piston in his engine moved back and forth. That swift-moving piston did a good job of pumping out flooded mines. He thought it might be useful in other ways too. He thought it might be connected to a wheel and used to operate many kinds of machinery.

Watt's other idea had to do with his engine's source of power. He was thinking about the possibility of making an engine in which steam alone provided all the energy that drove the piston back and forth. Watt was thinking of building, instead of an atmospheric engine, a real *steam engine.*

The Watt Steam Engine

JAMES WATT KNEW that even the best atmospheric engine produced power only when the piston was being forced down into the vacuum. When the piston was moving back again, the engine was simply "coasting," and didn't produce any power at all. In an atmospheric engine only every second stroke of the piston was a *power stroke.*

Watt wanted to use steam to push the piston first in one direction and then in the other. Then he would have an engine in which every stroke was a power stroke. Such an engine, he thought, would be twice as powerful as an atmospheric engine.

The steam engine that Watt patented in 1783 proved that he had been right. It was called a *double-acting* engine. Valves let steam into its cylinder first at one end, then at the other. Each jet of steam pushed the piston. Each stroke was a power stroke. When Watt connected the piston to a wheel, he had a steady source of power to operate any kind of machinery.

The Watt double-acting steam engine was quickly put to work in many ways. It was installed in spinning and weaving mills, in sawmills, in iron foundries and forges, in mines, and in city water-pumping stations. A manufacturer no longer had to depend on water power to turn his machines. He no longer had to build his factory beside a stream. Now he could erect a steam-powered factory at the most convenient place—near the source of his raw materials, perhaps, or at the edge of a town where he could hire plenty of workmen.

Watt's double-acting steam engine, in factories as well as mines, played a major part in the Industrial Revolution.

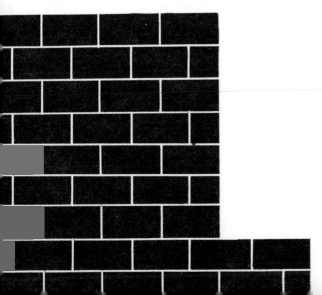

Factories became much more profitable. A great many new ones were built.

Machines in factories began to make many of the things that men had always made by hand. The period is called the Industrial Revolution, because industry began to change man's way of living. The Industrial Revolution took place gradually over many years. No one can say exactly when it started, because no one knows when the first factory was built. But the Industrial

Revolution began to make really important changes in men's lives only after factories became common. And this happened only after the development of a really dependable source of power that could be used anywhere. That source of power was James Watt's double-acting steam engine. So today we usually say that the Industrial Revolution began when Watt invented that engine.

Watt became prosperous. He and his partner received many orders for Watt engines. Watt had to spend a great deal of time talking to customers about the size of engine that would best suit their needs. He soon realized that it was difficult to explain just how much power one of his engines would produce. It was difficult because at that time no one had yet invented a method of measuring power.

So Watt himself invented a power-measuring method. He couldn't patent it. It never earned him any money. But even if he had never invented his steam engine, he would still be remembered today because he invented the unit of measurement we call the *horsepower*.

To understand horsepower, it is necessary to know the special meanings which scientists and engineers give to three ordinary words—*energy*, *work*, and *power*.

Energy, Work, and Power

THE WORDS *energy*, *work*, and *power* are often used in everyday conversation. Then they have what we might call everyday meanings.

You say, for example, "I played ball so long that I didn't have enough energy left to walk home." When you use *energy* in this way, you use it to mean strength.

You tell a friend, "I can't go to the library now because I have work to do at home." Here the word *work* means a task. It might be a physical task, such as mowing the lawn, or a mental task, such as solving arithmetic problems.

Or you say, "That bulldozer has a lot of power." You mean that the bulldozer can do hard work—pushing heavy boulders or gouging deeply into the earth. Here you are using *power* to express one of the several meanings a dictionary gives for this word: "Force or energy used to do work." That "force or energy" is the power talked about in this book. Usually when the word *power* is used in these pages, it has that meaning.

But when a physicist uses the words *power*, *work*, and *energy*, he has in mind a meaning different from the one people usually give those words in ordinary conversation.

Energy

ENERGY, TO A PHYSICIST, is the ability to change things or move things. It can take several different forms.

Whenever you move any part of your body, you are using what a scientist would call *muscular energy*. Energy harnessed to a machine is called *mechanical energy*. When scientists learned how to split an atom, they discovered *atomic energy*. Electricity, heat, sound, light, and chemical action represent still other forms of energy.

Energy can be changed from one form to another. If you rub two pieces of wood together, hard enough and long enough, you will set the wood aglow. When you

When an Indian made fire by rubbing two sticks together, he was changing muscular energy into heat energy.

do that, you are changing muscular energy—the energy of your own muscles—into *heat energy*.

If you drive a nail with a hammer, you first change the muscular energy in your arm into a form of energy possessed by moving things. Then, when the moving hammer strikes the nail, part of the energy it has drives the nail into the wood, and part is changed into heat energy. It is this heat energy that make the head of the nail hot after it has been struck many times.

When an electric current flows through a thin wire in a glass bulb, its energy changes to heat energy and *light energy*. This happens every time we turn on an electric light.

When we apply heat energy to water, and change the water into steam that drives an engine, we have changed heat energy into *mechanical energy*.

When the chemicals inside a flashlight battery act on each other to produce an electric current, *chemical energy* is being changed into *electrical energy*.

When sound waves strike a microphone in a broadcasting station, *sound energy* is changed into electrical energy. Then, if you tune in to that station, your loudspeaker changes the electrical energy back into sound energy again, so that you hear music or a speaker's voice.

Rays of sunlight focused through a magnifying glass onto a piece of paper may set the paper afire. The sun's light energy—called *radiant energy*, because it spreads out from the sun in rays—has changed into heat energy.

All around us, every moment of every day, energy is being changed from one form into another. Whenever energy is applied, it either changes something, or moves something, or causes both change and motion. That's why scientists say that energy is the ability to change or move things.

Work

A SCIENTIST SAYS that *work* is being done only when energy causes something to be moved.

The muscular energy you use to hammer a nail, for example, is producing work of the kind a physicist means when he uses this word. But part of your muscular energy is changed into heat energy that makes the nail head grow warm under your hammer blows. That part of your energy is not producing what a physicist means by work.

When you hammer a nail into wood, a scientist would say that you are doing work.

Electrical energy turning an electric motor, and heat energy spinning a steam turbine, are other examples of what a physicist means by work.

Power

ACCORDING TO its scientific definition, *power* is the rate at which work is being done. The word has to do not only with the amount of work that is being done, but also with the length of time it takes.

The difference between the everyday meaning of the word *power* and its scientific meaning is not always easy to understand. James Watt understood it. When he said he wanted to be able to measure power, he was using the word in the same way a scientist uses it today in his laboratory.

James Watt was a practical man. He realized that many of the customers for his steam engines knew very little about them. So he decided to base a power-measuring unit on something they would be sure to understand. He based it on the amount of work a strong horse could do in a certain length of time.

He knew it was important to make time a part of his unit. He might have explained it this way:

Suppose 10 bags of potatoes are lying on the sidewalk, outside a grocery store, where the delivery truck dumped them. Each bag weighs 25 pounds. The store owner must decide whether to carry the bags into the

store himself, or ask his delivery boy to do it. The owner can pick up two bags at once. He will be able to carry all the bags into the store in five trips. But his young delivery boy is able to carry only a single bag, and will have to make ten trips to carry all the bags into the store. Each will have to do the same amount of work in order to finish the job by himself. Each will have to carry a total of 250 pounds of potatoes. But the store owner can do it himself in half the time the boy will need.

Therefore, James Watt might have said, the store owner is twice as *powerful* as his delivery boy.

Horsepower

To FIGURE OUT his power-measurement unit, Watt rigged up a series of pulleys and threaded a heavy rope through them. He fastened a weight to one end of the rope. He hitched a horse to the other. Then, when the horse moved forward, the weight was lifted up off the ground.

Watt found that the horse could raise a 3,300-pound weight ten feet into the air in one minute.

If Watt had added more pulleys to his rigging, so that the weight rose more slowly, the horse could have lifted ten times that weight, or 33,000 pounds. But in one minute the horse would have lifted that weight only one foot off the ground instead of ten feet.

Watt gave the name *horsepower* to the amount of work the horse was doing in one minute—whether the animal was lifting 3,300 pounds ten feet into the air, or lifting 33,000 pounds one foot into the air. Watt wrote down the definition of this new unit of measurement like this:

1 *horsepower* = 33,000 *foot-pounds per minute*

If one of Watt's engines could lift 330,000 pounds one foot in one minute, he called it a 10-horsepower engine.

For more than a hundred years, Watt's double-acting steam engine supplied most of the world's mechanical power. It ran factories. It propelled ocean liners and steam locomotives. It powered steam rollers, steam shovels, and threshing machines.

Then the situation began to change. Men were constantly finding new tasks for mechanical power to perform. For some of these tasks the Watt engine was too heavy, or too slow, or too expensive to operate. Other tasks demanded more power than even the biggest steam engine could supply. To fill these new power needs, inventors began to produce new kinds of engines. Some of these new engines also operated on steam. Others operated on oil or gasoline. And as these new engines appeared, steam engines began to vanish. Today very few are still in use.

But the method that Watt invented to measure the

Watt measured the power of engines in terms of horsepower.

power of his engines is just as important today as ever. All newer engines that have replaced his steam engine are still rated by the unit he named the horsepower. And many years after Watt's death other scientists honored him by giving his name to the unit by which we measure electric power. Whenever we speak of a 100-watt bulb, we are using the name of the man who invented that first useful method for measuring power.

Energy From the Sun

EVERY MINUTE OF EVERY DAY, mankind uses tremendous quantities of energy. Most of it comes from one source—the sun.

The muscular energy you use when you pick up this book, for example, comes from the sun. It reaches your muscles by a long process.

1. The sun shines on plants. Let's say, in this case, the sun shines on a field of peas. The *radiant energy* of the sun is applied to the green pea plants.

2. The sun's radiant energy changes certain substances inside the plants—substances which the plants have obtained from air or water or soil—into sugar. The plants then contain the *chemical energy* of the sugar.

3. You eat peas from that field. Your body then contains the sugar's chemical energy.

4. Inside your body the process of digestion changes that chemical energy into *muscular energy*—the energy you use when you pick up this book. (Some of the chemical energy may be changed into *heat energy*, too, to keep you from freezing on a cold day.)

Of course you don't get all of your muscular energy from peas or other plants. You get some of it from

Energy for work and play comes from the sun.

meat and milk and butter and eggs. But all of those products come from animals, and those animals live on plants. So when you eat a hamburger, or drink a glass of milk, you are adding one more step to the long process that brings you energy from the sun. In that case the sun's energy goes first to plants, then to an animal, and then to you.

Each time you breathe, each time your heart beats, you are using muscular energy that was once radiant energy from the sun, 93,000,000 miles away.

When we use water power we are also using energy that originally came from the sun.

The process begins when the sun's rays strike the ocean and other bodies of water. In the water the sun's radiant energy turns to heat energy. This heat energy evaporates the water—that is, turns it into an invisible gas called water vapor. That gas rises upward until it meets the cold upper air, and there it cools and turns back into water again. That water falls on the earth as rain or snow. And the water from rain or snow, flowing down the earth's hills back toward the sea, forms brooks and rivers. It is those downward-flowing streams that turn water wheels.

The radiant energy of the sun, heating the surface of the earth, is also responsible for the energy that propels sailboats and turns windmills. When the earth's surface becomes hot, it heats the air above it. The hotter that air becomes, the lighter it grows. As it grows lighter it rises. As it rises it leaves space for cooler, heavier air around it to move in and take its place—and to grow hot in its turn and rise upward.

That sideways movement of heavy, cool air is what we call wind.

The mechanical energy that drives our cars also comes from the sun, by a process that took millions of years. That process began when the sun's radiant energy turned into chemical energy inside countless tiny plants growing in prehistoric times. Those plants, or the tiny animals that ate those plants, died and decayed millions of years ago. But that chemical energy remained in their decayed bodies. Those bodies were gradually covered up by layers of rock and soil, and were transformed into oil. And the oil, too, had that same chemical energy.

Today we bring oil up out of the earth and refine it to get gasoline. Then the engines of our cars transform that chemical energy into mechanical energy to turn a car's wheels.

When we burn oil to heat houses, we are transforming the oil's chemical energy into heat energy. And when we burn coal, which was created in much the same way oil was created, we are again making use of the radiant energy of the sun. Those fuels which have been buried for millions of years are called *fossil fuels*.

Until our own century, men knew of only two kinds of energy that didn't come from the sun. One was the energy of the tides. The other was the energy from the molten inner core of the earth. Up to now man has not used either of these very much, though he may make much greater use of them in the future.

But today man knows about a third kind of energy which does not come from the sun, and he is already beginning to use it. This is the energy found inside the tiny particle of matter we call the *atom*.

7

Energy From Atoms

MORE THAN TWO THOUSAND YEARS AGO a Greek named Democritus had an idea that sounded very strange to the people of his time. He believed that everything he could see—plants, animals, people, stones, water, and the very earth itself—was made up of tiny particles much too small to be seen. Each of these particles, Democritus said, was so small that it couldn't possibly be cut into smaller parts even with the sharpest knife. He named the particles *atomos*, the Greek word for uncuttable.

Today we know that Democritus was on the right

track. We still use the word *atom*, from the Greek *atomos*, to describe the invisible particles that make up everything on our earth. All matter, scientists believe, is composed of atoms which are usually clumped together to form the larger particles we call *molecules*.

Democritus was right when he said that atoms are very tiny particles. Modern experts have figured out that one ounce of hydrogen gas contains 17,500,000,000,000,-000,000,000,000 atoms—17 septillion, 500 sextillion atoms.

But today we know that Democritus was wrong when he said that an atom was uncuttable. Scientists have discovered that each atom is made up of still tinier particles, and that atoms can be "split" or "smashed." The process of atom splitting is called *atomic fission*.

In order to understand something of what happens in atomic fission it is necessary to know something about the particles that make up the atom.

The Particles of the Atom

THE PARTICLES THAT MAKE UP the atom are called *protons*, *neutrons*, and *electrons*. All protons are exactly alike. All neutrons are exactly alike. All electrons are exactly alike. But two atoms may be different from each other because they contain different numbers of protons, neutrons, and electrons.

An atom of helium, for example, contains two protons, two neutrons, and two electrons. An atom of

The Library
Special Childrens Collection
Saint Francis College
Fort Wayne, Indiana

uranium-238 contains 92 protons, 146 neutrons, and 92 electrons. The helium atom is very light because it contains so few particles. A uranium atom is much heavier because it contains so many more particles. Scientists use the word *mass* when they talk about the quantity of matter in two such atoms. They say that a helium atom has less mass than a uranium atom.

The protons in each atom, clinging together with the particles called neutrons, make up the atom's central core, or kernel. That core is called the *nucleus*, a word that comes from the Latin word for kernel. (The plural of nucleus is *nuclei*.) The electrons, very much lighter than protons and neutrons, whirl around the nucleus in much the same way that planets whirl around the sun.

Men Learn About the Atom

UNTIL THE 1890's, most scientists agreed with Democritus. They believed that the atom was the smallest particle of matter there was, and that it was uncuttable.

But about that time a French scientist, Henri Becquerel, discovered a strange thing about uranium. He discovered that this material gave off invisible rays which darkened a photographic plate, just as ordinary light rays do.

One of Becquerel's students, a young Polish girl named Marie Sklodowska, began to study these invisible rays. When Marie married a French physicist, Pierre

Marie and Pierre Curie studied radioactive atoms.

Curie, he joined her in her work. Together they carried out many experiments with uranium. They were trying to learn more about the invisible rays it gives off.

Everyone knows one result of the Curies' work. They discovered radium.

But their work was important for another reason too. When they became sure that those rays came from inside the tiny atoms of uranium, they began to doubt that a uranium atom was a single solid piece of matter.

Their new curiosity about atoms made other people

curious about them too. Out of that curiosity a new science was born—the science of atomic physics.

Before long two atomic particles were discovered: the proton and the electron. (The neutron was not discovered until 1932.) A few years later scientists also discovered that some uranium atoms break down, or split, sending out two particles and a ray of invisible light. Scientists realized that that ray was what had darkened the photographic plates in Becquerel's laboratory.

Scientists use the word *radioactive* to describe uranium, radium, and any other materials that can radiate particles and rays. They named the two particles *alpha* and *beta*. They named the ray *gamma*. The three names come from the first three letters of the Greek alphabet.

Those radiating gamma rays are a form of energy, just as visible light rays are a form of energy. The alpha and beta particles, shooting out of the atom's nucleus at high speed, also possess energy because of their motion.

When scientists had discovered those two particles and the gamma ray, they knew that the atom releases energy.

Immediately, then, people began to ask two questions.

The first was: Does the atom itself create the energy it releases and, if not, where does that energy come from?

The second question was: How can mankind make practical use of this newly discovered atomic energy?

No one could answer the second question until the

first had been answered. In order to put atomic energy to work, it was first necessary to know how it came into existence, so that it could be produced in quantities big enough to be useful.

Where Atomic Energy Comes From

ONLY PEOPLE WHO KNEW nothing about science dared to say, "It is clear where atomic energy comes from. It is simply created inside an atom."

Scientists refused to say that. They had learned, as part of their training, that energy can be neither created nor destroyed. They believed that energy can only be changed from one form to another. They believed that no energy is either gained or lost when such a change takes place. Those beliefs formed one of the basic laws of chemistry and physics. It is called the *law of the conservation of energy*.

But for some time no one could explain where atomic energy does come from, if it is not created inside an atom. Finally, early in the twentieth century, a satisfactory explanation was suggested by a German-born mathematician and physicist. This man, who became one of the most famous and best-loved men in the world, was Albert Einstein.

Einstein did not ignore the law of the conservation of energy. Instead he combined that law with another one, known as the *law of the conservation of matter*.

As Albert Einstein explained, some matter in an atom's nucleus may be changed into energy.

This law says that matter, like energy, can never be created or destroyed, but only changed from one form to another. A piece of burning wood, according to this law, is not destroyed by fire. Instead it is transformed into ashes, carbon, and gas. All the atoms in the original piece of wood have become part of other matter. Nothing has been lost.

This is how Einstein explained atomic energy: Energy and matter, he said, are different forms of the same thing. If matter is "destroyed," he said, energy is created. If energy is "destroyed," matter is created. Neither one is ever really lost, even when it no longer seems to exist. Instead, it has been transformed into the other.

Therefore, Einstein said, when a radioactive atom

seems to "create" energy, this is what is really happening: Some of the matter of the atom's nucleus is being transformed into energy.

Putting Atomic Energy to Work

IT WAS ONE THING TO KNOW that a radioactive atom sometimes shot particles out of its nucleus—swiftly moving particles that possessed energy. It was quite another thing to produce enough of this energy to do even small jobs—jobs that electrical energy was already doing cheaply and efficiently.

Scientists tried many different methods to make radioactive atoms release energy quickly and in large quantities. They tried to "break down" atoms with heat, with cold, with pressure, and with heavy blows. None of those attempts succeeded.

Finally a British physicist, Ernest Rutherford, discovered that a shooting alpha particle, striking against an atom of nitrogen, could break that atom down. When this happened, one proton shot out of the nitrogen atom. And that shooting proton had more energy than the shooting alpha particle that had jarred it loose.

The energy of the shooting alpha particle had acted as a "bullet." When it struck the nitrogen atom it "knocked off" a proton—and released more energy.

Other scientists picked up Rutherford's clue, and tried to carry his work further. They invented electric-powered machines that could "fire" protons and other kinds of "bullets" at atomic targets. The cyclotron, the synchrotron, and the betatron are among the "bullet-firing" machines that are sometimes called "atom smashers." They are very valuable for atomic research.

But an atom smasher isn't a very efficient machine. Each time it fires a million proton "bullets," only one of those protons may strike an atom squarely enough to chip off some of its particles and thus release more energy. The machine never produces as much energy as it uses up, in the form of electrical energy, for its operation.

Then the atomic particles called neutrons were discovered in 1932. They proved to be far better bullets than protons. They made more hits.

One day, in a German laboratory, several physicists were bombarding uranium atoms with neutrons. That day they made a surprising discovery. They discovered that when a neutron struck the nucleus of a uranium atom, it didn't simply drive off a few particles. Instead it actually split the uranium nucleus into two almost equal parts which shot apart at high speed. The shooting parts of the split atom had far more energy than a shooting alpha particle, or a shooting proton, or a shooting neutron.

That neutron bombardment, as it is called, had released more energy than had ever before been released by striking a single atom. But the process of bringing about the bombardment still used up more energy than it released.

Those German scientists, and others who soon copied their experiments, were using a kind of uranium called uranium-238. The number indicates that the nucleus of this material contains a total of 238 particles—92 protons and 146 neutrons. But very soon scientists began to experiment with another kind of uranium called uranium-235, whose nucleus contains only 235 particles. This material is much rarer than uranium-238, and therefore very costly. But it proved to be worth its high price. It was this material that finally opened the way to the large-scale production of atomic energy.

The two kinds of uranium are quite similar in some ways. An atom of each one divides into two smaller atoms when it is "split," and in each case energy is released. But in two important ways the two kinds of uranium are different.

Uranium-235 atoms can be split more easily than their close chemical relatives. Only a high-speed neutron can penetrate an atom of uranium-238. But a slower-moving neutron can penetrate an atom of uranium-235 and split its nucleus.

The second difference between the two is that a split atom of uranium-235 not only forms two smaller atoms, but also shoots out several extra neutrons at the same time.

The Chain Reaction

THIS IS WHAT HAPPENS—under certain conditions —in a lump of uranium-235:

The nucleus of an atom of uranium-235 picks up a stray neutron and splits. It releases some energy, and also shoots out several extra neutrons.

A few of those extra neutrons make square hits on other atoms of the uranium. These atoms split and release more energy and more extra neutrons.

These neutrons, in turn, strike still more atoms, releasing still more energy and still more neutrons.

The process speeds up as it continues, and it is easy to see why. If the first atom releases two extra neutrons, and they strike two atoms, the result is four extra neutrons. If these four strike four more atoms, the result is eight extra neutrons. Then the number increases to 16, to 32, and so on. Because the splitting of each nucleus is a link in the chain of nuclear splitting, or *nuclear fission*, as it is called, this process is known as a *chain reaction*.

If all the nuclear fission in a chain reaction takes place very quickly—in a few millionths of a second— the billions and billions of splitting nuclei release their energy in one huge explosive blast. This kind of blast,

When a neutron hits a uranium-235 nucleus, the atom splits into two fragments and several neutrons. This can lead to a chain reaction.

powerful enough to destroy everything within miles, is what occurs when an atomic bomb explodes.

But if the chain reaction is controlled, so that all the uranium nuclei do not split at almost the same instant, the energy is released more slowly. Then the heat generated by the motion energy of the nuclear fragments can be put to work, just as we put to work the heat energy from oil or coal.

To start a chain reaction it is necessary to have a piece of uranium which contains enough atoms to guarantee targets for the flying neutrons. The smallest piece of uranium that will provide enough targets is called the *critical mass*.

To set off an atomic bomb, two lumps of uranium are used. Each lump is smaller than the critical mass. By itself it would not start a chain reaction. The two lumps, kept apart, are no more dangerous than two lumps of lead. But if the lumps are jammed together into one, they make a lump big enough to reach the critical mass—big enough to set off an atomic explosion.

The discovery of a way to split atomic nuclei gave the world a more terrible weapon than any known before in history. The same discovery also gave the world a new source of energy so important that the age we live in is sometimes called the Atomic Age.

But to use atomic energy in peaceful ways requires engines that can turn energy into useful work. Some of the devices that can do this are, as we shall see, even

newer than the discovery of atomic energy itself. Others—
the turbine, the electric generator, the electric motor—
are not new at all. They were developed in the nineteenth
century.

8

The Turbine

THE FIRST IMPORTANT new power-producing machine of the nineteenth century was the *turbine*. Its name comes from the Latin word *turbo*, meaning something that spins. Its invention, like that of the steam engine, resulted from the efforts of many men to solve a particular problem.

The problem arose when people realized that the steam engine was not really practical under all conditions. Operating a steam engine at the head of a coal mine was both cheap and efficient. The coal for heating the water in the engine's boiler was right at hand. But when a man built an iron foundry, say, hundreds of miles from the nearest coal mine, he could not obtain steam power cheaply. He had to pay too much to bring coal to his foundry by horse-drawn wagon or by one of the few new railroads of that day. So if a river ran past his foundry he usually decided to use water power instead of a steam engine. In many parts of the world the water wheel was still the best and cheapest source of power.

But men were becoming dissatisfied with the ordinary water wheel. They were learning how inefficient it was. The water that poured onto the wheel usually overflowed the buckets. This meant that a lot of water simply poured past the wheel and ran off without having done any work.

The Water Turbine

SEVERAL MEN, working at about the same time, tried to cut down on the waste of water by building a cover around a water wheel. But their enclosed wheels weren't much more efficient than an open wheel.

Then, about 1830, Benoit Fourneyron, a Frenchman, made a wheel with curved blades. He set it inside a covering that was also fitted with curved blades on its inner walls. The wheel was called a *rotor*. The covering was called a *housing*. Fourneyron had made the most

Hydro-electric plants, using water turbines, provide about one-third of the world's electric power.

efficient enclosed water wheel that had ever been built. He had made the first *turbine*.

When water entered the turbine, the housing's curved blades set it whirling, like the water in a whirlpool. This whirling motion did two things: It increased the speed of the water's flow, and it directed the water against the rotor's curved blades at an angle that increased its push. The turbine made good use both of the water's speed and of its weight.

Fourneyron's first little turbine produced only 6 horsepower. His second was almost twice as powerful. His third, built to operate the mechanical hammers in an iron foundry, produced 50 horsepower. It was so successful that soon men in other countries were building turbines too. Not all of them were just like Fourneyron's, but they operated in much the same way.

The new water turbines were smooth-running and efficient. Built near a good water supply, they produced cheap and dependable power. By 1850 they were in operation along the rivers and streams of both Europe and the United States. Half a century later, when men had discovered how to produce electricity, water turbines found their biggest and most useful task: They were put to work turning the great electric generators in hydro-electric power stations.

The word *hydro-electric*, which means water-electric, refers to the process of changing the energy of falling water into electrical energy. The water in the 115-mile lake behind Hoover Dam, on the Colorado River, operates eighteen enormous turbines in a big hydro-electric station below the dam. Those eighteen turbines produce enough electricity for a city of 7,500,000 people.

The water turbine—an enclosed water wheel—is far more efficient than the old open wheel.

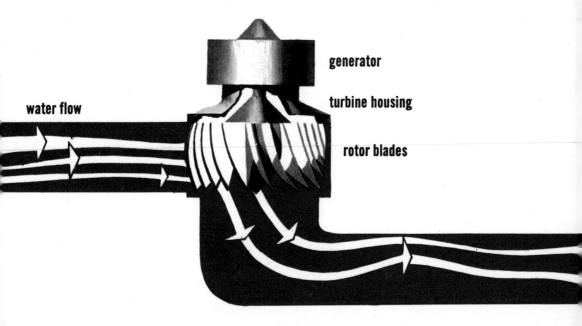

generator

turbine housing

water flow

rotor blades

The Steam Turbine

AFTER FOURNEYRON LEARNED how to make an efficient water turbine, he tried to make a similar machine driven by steam.

Fourneyron failed, and so did the other men who tried the same thing at the same time. They failed because steam moves with great speed—far faster than water tumbling down from a height. And in Fourneyron's day no one knew how to construct a turbine so strong and so accurately balanced that it wouldn't fly apart at high speed.

Then stronger steel was developed. Machinists improved their skill and accuracy. And in 1884, in England, a man named Charles A. Parsons built a different kind of steam turbine. His was successful.

The rotor of Parsons' turbine didn't have blades arranged in a single row like the blades of a water turbine. Instead it had many rows of curved blades, all fastened to the turbine's shaft, or axle. The housing also had many rows of blades, curved in the opposite direction to those on the rotor, and arranged to fit between the rows of rotor blades. This meant that the entire housing was filled with blades. First came a row of stationary blades attached to the housing, then a row of movable blades attached to the rotor, then another row of sta-

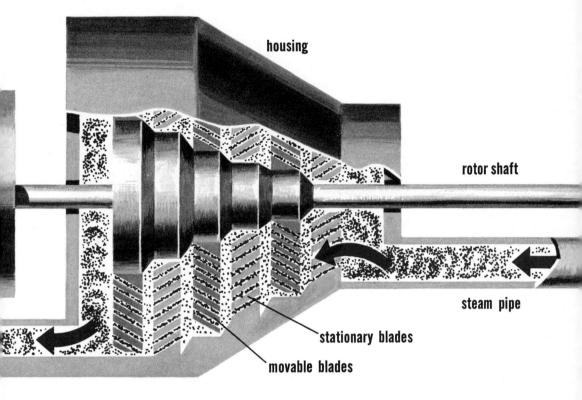

Steam turbines produce about two-thirds of the world's electricity.

tionary blades, and so on. All the blades were slanted
in such a way that when steam entered the turbine, it
zigzagged from one row to the next. Each time the
steam struck a row of movable blades, it pushed against
them and made them move.

In this kind of turbine, very little of the steam's
heat and pressure is wasted. A Newcomen engine used
about 20 pounds of coal to produce one horsepower.
A good Watt engine used 6 pounds of coal for the

same purpose. But a modern steam turbine can produce that much power for less than 1 pound of coal.

Steam turbines and water turbines have three advantages over steam engines.

First, turbines operate more cheaply than steam engines.

Second, turbines operate more smoothly than steam engines. A turbine has no parts that move back and forth like the piston of a steam engine. The turbine rotates steadily.

Third, turbines can be built so large that they can produce more power than steam engines. The largest Watt-type steam engine produced about 10,000 horsepower. Turbines have been built large enough to produce 300,000 horsepower.

Steam and water turbines are today's largest sources of mechanical power. Without them it would be difficult and expensive to generate all the electricity the world needs.

The Gas Turbine

A STEAM TURBINE is driven by the hot high-pressure gas we call steam. That gas is produced outside the turbine, in a boiler, by heating water.

A newer kind of turbine is driven by hot high-pressure gases produced right inside the turbine. The gases are produced by burning a mixture of air and kerosene or some similar fuel.

When gas turbines turn an airplane's propellers, they are called turbo-prop *engines.*

This *gas turbine*, as it is called, has several other parts besides its rotor and housing. One is an air pump, or *air compressor*. This consists of rows of curved blades like the blades of the rotor, fastened to the same shaft that carries the rotor's blades. The air compressor's blades are on one end of the shaft. The rotor's blades are on the other. A gas turbine also has a *combustion chamber*, between the air compressor and the rotor. It is in this chamber that the mixture of air and fuel is burned.

The turning blades of the air compressor force air into the combustion chamber. There fuel is added and the fuel-air mixture is set afire by a spark. The great quantities of very hot high-pressure gases that are produced escape through the rear of the housing. On their way out they push against the curved blades of the turbine rotor, and keep it spinning.

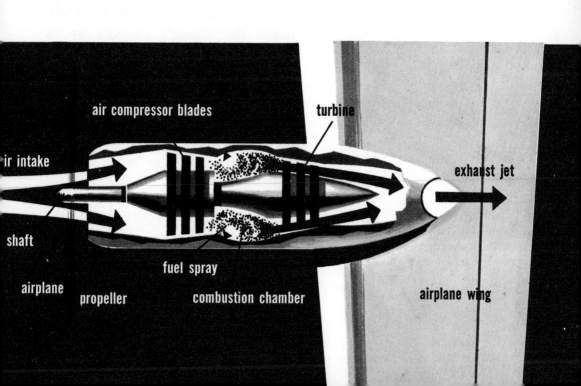

Gas turbines turn the propellers of many airplanes. When they are used for that purpose they are called *turbo-prop engines*.

Gas turbines also operate pumps. They have been tested as engines for trucks, automobiles, and boats. They operate steadily and without vibration, but they make loud whistling noises and shoot out dangerous blasts of hot gases. Engineers are working to find ways to muffle a gas turbine's noise, and to devise methods for releasing the exhaust gases safely. When gas turbines are made quieter and safer, they will be used in many ways.

One great advantage of the gas turbine is that it is very small in comparison to the amount of power it produces. A gas turbine powerful enough to drive a big truck would be about the size of a small barrel.

The gas turbine belongs to a family of engines known as *internal-combustion* engines. All the engines in this family are driven by the energy of hot gases produced by burning fuel right inside the engine's cylinder or its combustion chamber. The gas turbine is a new member of this family. The most familiar internal-combustion engines are gasoline engines and Diesel engines.

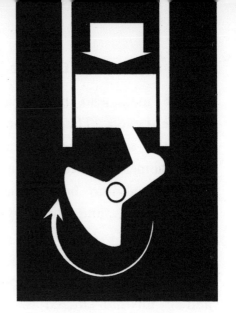

9

Gasoline Engines and Diesel Engines

EARLY IN THE NINETEENTH CENTURY, many inventors had the idea of using burning or exploding fuel to push an engine's piston back and forth. If steam can do it, they said, why not other kinds of hot gases?

Some men believed that the gases from exploding gunpowder could be used to move a piston just as they move a bullet in a gun barrel. Others wanted to try explosive gases such as hydrogen. But nobody succeeded in building a really useful internal-combustion engine until about 1860.

The man who built that engine was a Frenchman, Etienne Lenoir. The fuel he used was a gas made from coal, the same kind of gas now used for cooking in many homes. In Lenoir's day that gas was just beginning to be piped into houses, here and there, to supply fuel for gas lights and stoves.

In Lenoir's engine the gas was mixed with air. The air was necessary because it contains oxygen. Nothing will burn except in the presence of oxygen. The gas-and-air mixture entered the engine's cylinder and was set afire. This produced hot gases which pushed against the piston and moved it first one way and then the other.

The four steps in the operation of an Otto engine, which burned gas.
The gasoline engine of today works in much the same way.

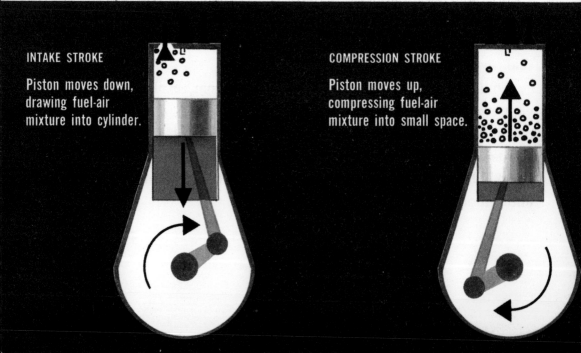

INTAKE STROKE

Piston moves down, drawing fuel-air mixture into cylinder.

COMPRESSION STROKE

Piston moves up, compressing fuel-air mixture into small space.

The hot gases did what the steam did in Watt's steam engine.

Lenoir's engine had one great advantage. It was small. Many men had been looking for a small engine that could do the light jobs for which a steam engine was too big and heavy. Soon several hundred Lenoir engines had been sold in France and England.

Lenoir's engine wasn't very good, however. It often broke down. It also operated very inefficiently. It used enormous amounts of fuel for the 3 horsepower it produced.

But it did convince people that small internal-combustion engines might be built that would operate both successfully and economically.

The first man who actually built such an engine was Nicholas Otto, a German engineer. He worked on it

POWER STROKE
Fuel-air mixture is exploded. Hot gases push piston down.

EXHAUST STROKE
Piston moves up, pushing gases out of cylinder.

for years. When he was finally successful, he declared that his engine "worked so beautifully and so elegantly that it would have given an angel joy to watch it."

In most important ways the Otto engine, built in 1876, was like the gasoline engines used today. It had five important parts:

1. A cylinder.

2. A piston.

3. A crankshaft connected to the piston.

4. Valves which opened to admit fresh fuel and to allow the gases to escape after they had pushed against the piston.

5. A device to explode the fuel-air mixture.

The four steps in the operation of the Otto engine form what engineers call a *cycle of operation*. When the engine completed one cycle, it started another. Since the piston moved one stroke for each step of the cycle, the Otto engine became known as a 4-stroke cycle engine.

Otto's engine was a great success. It used only half as much fuel as Lenoir's engine and was far more dependable. It was simpler to operate than a steam engine. It could be installed fairly easily wherever a supply of gas was available.

The Gasoline Engine

OF COURSE many factory owners said, "The Otto engine is useless to me. No gas is piped into the neighborhood of my factory."

And other men who were dreaming of making horseless carriages said, "The Otto engine is useless to us. We want an engine that is even lighter than this one. And we need an engine that operates on some kind of fuel that can be carried right in a carriage—a liquid fuel, perhaps, that could be carried in a tank attached to the carriage."

Those men began to study the liquid fuels that were then known. One of these fuels was petroleum—the crude oil itself, just as it came out of the ground, and the substances that could be made out of it. Kerosene was the only such substance that had any real value in those days. The other substances in petroleum were usually thrown away after the kerosene used for lamps had been taken out of the oil.

Finally the men who were dreaming of horseless carriages decided that one of those thrown-away substances might be what they were looking for. This was the substance we now call gasoline. (Often we call it *gas* even though it is a liquid.) Gasoline evaporates—changes into a vapor or gas—very rapidly. When gasoline

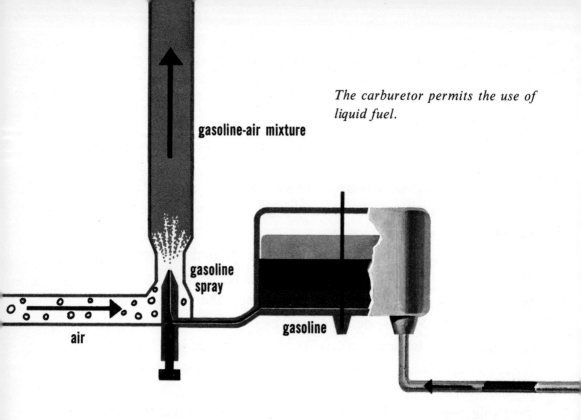

gasoline-air mixture

The carburetor permits the use of liquid fuel.

gasoline
spray

air

gasoline

vapor was mixed with air it could be exploded very easily to produce hot gases.

Several men tried to build an engine in which gasoline could be vaporized and mixed with air. In 1882 one of them succeeded. Like Otto, he was a German engineer. His name was Gottlieb Daimler.

Daimler's 4-stroke engine could use the power of exploding gasoline because it had a device called a *carburetor*. This important device sprayed the liquid fuel into the air which the engine sucked up. The droplets of gasoline that emerged from the carburetor were so tiny that they evaporated instantly, combining with the air to form an explosive mixture.

Daimler's engine laid the foundation for the giant automobile industry. Daimler himself made a horseless carriage that was one of the world's early automobiles. Later the engine he developed made the airplane possible too. And today that engine supplies power for hundreds of purposes wherever gasoline is sold.

Gasoline engines have been improved tremendously since Gottlieb Daimler built his first model. Today's engines are quieter, longer-lasting, more efficient, and much more powerful. The early engines could produce only 3 or 4 horsepower. Some present-day automobile engines produce more than 300 horsepower, and some airplane engines produce 2,000 horsepower.

Today's gasoline engines can also be made much lighter than the early models. Some weigh only fifteen or twenty pounds, and are used to power lawn mowers, saws, and other types of portable equipment. Some of these very light engines operate on a 2-stroke cycle, and are generally called 2-cycle engines.

The Diesel Engine

AT ABOUT THE SAME TIME that Daimler was building his first gasoline-driven automobiles, another German engineer named Rudolph Diesel was experimenting with engines. He was trying to build an internal-combustion engine powerful enough to do some of the heavy jobs that steam engines were then doing. He wanted to make engines that would produce several hundred horsepower to propel ships, to pump water for cities, to operate hoists in mines, and to run ore crushers.

Diesel didn't plan to run his engine on gasoline. At first he thought of trying to use coal dust because it was so cheap. But his coal-dust engine blew up, and Diesel almost lost his life. Next he planned to use the cheap, heavier-than-gasoline oils that came out of petroleum. To get as much power as possible out of the oil, he intended to compress his fuel-air mixture twice as much as the mixture was compressed in gasoline engines.

Again Diesel ran into a serious obstacle. When gas is compressed, it becomes hot. The more it is compressed,

The four steps in the operation of a Diesel engine, which burns oil.

INTAKE STROKE

Piston moves down,
drawing air into cylinder.

COMPRESSION STROKE

Piston moves up,
compressing and heating air.

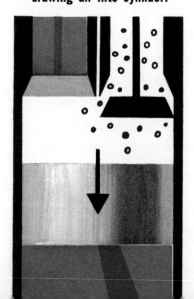
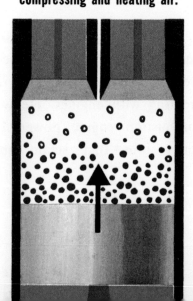

the hotter it grows. And the pressure inside the cylinder of Diesel's engine was very great. It caused the fuel to explode from its own heat before the piston reached the top of its compression stroke. This meant that the piston was driven back down, by the force of that explosion, before it had completed its upstroke. And that downward "kick" of the piston forced the crankshaft to turn backward.

Finally Diesel worked out a method to overcome that obstacle. His engine sucked nothing but air into the bottom of its cylinder. Therefore, as the piston moved upward, it was compressing nothing but air. Compressed air becomes very hot, but it does not explode. So there was no danger of an explosion at the wrong moment.

POWER STROKE

Oil sprayed into hot compressed air explodes, pushing piston down.

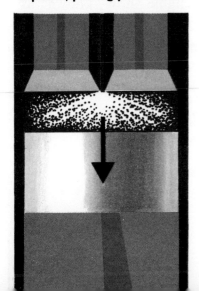

EXHAUST STROKE

Piston moves up, pushing gases out of cylinder.

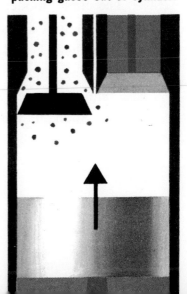

*The Diesel engine has replaced the Watt steam engine
on land and at sea.*

Then, when the piston reached the very top of its compression stroke, oil was sprayed into the cylinder—into
the hot compressed air. The fuel burned instantly, producing gases that drove the piston down on its power
stroke.

The first model of the engine now known as the
Diesel engine appeared in 1895. It did everything its
inventor had hoped it would do. It was a very heavy,
slow-turning engine. But it was tough and durable. It
was almost three times as efficient as a Watt steam
engine. Soon it was replacing that engine on land and
on sea.

Modern Diesels are still fairly heavy compared to modern gasoline engines. Diesel cylinders must be strong enough to withstand air pressure as high as 500 pounds per square inch. They must also be able to withstand temperatures of over 1,000 degrees. But with modern steel and other modern metals, a Diesel can now be made light enough and fast enough to be used in trucks and buses.

Today Diesel engines also provide power for tractors, road-building machinery, cranes, dredges, and railroad locomotives. Diesels now power many water-pumping stations and electric generating plants, too, and drive huge ships across the ocean. A Diesel in the engine room of an ocean liner may produce more than 20,000 horse-power.

10

Electric Generators and Electric Motors

ELECTRICAL ENERGY COMES from the whirling atomic particle we call an *electron*.

Once that name, electron, had a very different meaning. In ancient Greece *elektron* was the name used for amber, a yellowish hardened tree sap. Greeks used amber for beads and other ornaments, just as we do today. And a Greek named Thales, who lived about 2,500 years ago, made a discovery when he rubbed a piece of amber briskly with cloth. He found that amber would acquire the ability to attract dust and small bits of feathers.

Thales was probably the first man in history to notice one small example of the great source of power we call electricity.

More than two thousand years later an English scientist, William Gilbert, also noticed amber's ability to attract other objects. He called its strange ability *the electric*, from the Greek name for amber itself. And when Gilbert discovered that certain other things also had that same ability, he called them all "electrics." Some of those other "electrics" were hollow balls and rods of glass, and balls of sulphur.

In Gilbert's day, in the late 1500's, people were becoming interested in all sorts of scientific curiosities. Gilbert's "electrics" became popular scientific playthings. Men discovered that the "electrics" didn't always attract objects. Sometimes, instead, they repelled those same objects—pushed them away. Men also discovered that the "electrics" could give off sparks.

One famous German scientist, Otto von Guericke, put a large ball of sulphur on a rod which he could spin by turning a crank. As Von Guericke turned the crank with one hand, and held his other hand against the spinning ball, sparks flew out. He had built what might be called the first electric machine.

In 1746 a Dutch professor, Pieter van Musschenbroek, tried to put electricity into water—or, as we would say today, he tried to charge water with electricity. He put some water in a jar and closed the jar with a cork.

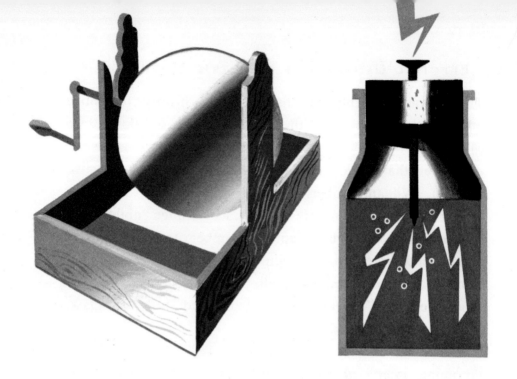

Von Guericke's electric machine (left). Leyden jar for storing electricity (right).

Then, through the cork, he poked a nail long enough to reach down into the water. Next he cranked up an electric machine—a machine like Von Guericke's, which could produce sparks—and held the head of the nail against the spinning ball. When he stopped the machine, he accidentally touched the nail head. Suddenly he found himself sprawling on the floor. The professor had been knocked off his feet by the violence of an electric shock. All the electricity that had been stored in the jar had leaped through him in one painful jolt.

Men soon discovered they could store electricity in

an empty jar that had been coated inside and out with a thin layer of lead. Such jars were called Leyden jars because they had first been made in the Dutch city of Leyden. Leyden jars became useful tools for further experiments.

When Benjamin Franklin sent a kite aloft during a thunderstorm, he held the kite string near the neck of a Leyden jar as the lightning flashed. The jar became charged with electricity. Franklin had proved that the little sparks from an electric machine were the same thing as the huge sparks we call lightning.

Franklin actually put electricity to work. He used it to prepare a turkey for a dinner party. He said the turkey was "killed by the *electrical shock*, and roasted by the *electrical jack*, before a fire kindled by the *electrified bottle*."

Most people thought Franklin's electrical devices were amusing toys and nothing more. But men went on experimenting with electricity out of curiosity, and trying to understand it. Sometimes a mistake made by one scientist gave another a useful clue.

An Italian doctor made that kind of mistake in 1780. Luigi Galvani wanted to see what effect electricity had on muscles. He discovered that the legs of a dead frog would twitch, just as if the frog were alive, when an electric machine was operating nearby. Then one day he took some frog legs out of the salt solution he kept them in, and attached them to copper hooks. He hung the hooks over an iron bar so that the legs would dry off. When one of the legs happened to touch the iron bar, it twitched—just as if it were close to a spinning electric machine. Galvani thought he had discovered a new kind of electricity. He called it animal electricity.

Another Italian, Alessandro Volta, didn't believe there was such a thing as animal electricity. Volta agreed that electricity had made those salt-soaked frog legs twitch. But he thought the electricity had somehow come from the salt and the copper and the iron in Galvani's equipment. Volta decided to prove his theory by bringing those three materials together in another way.

He got some sheets of iron and copper and piled them up—first an iron sheet, then a copper sheet, and so on. Between each pair of copper and iron sheets he put a piece of leather that had been soaked in salt water. Then he put one hand on the copper sheet on the top of the pile, and the other hand on the iron sheet at the bottom of the pile. Instantly he felt a shock of electricity run through his body from one hand to the other. He had proved that salt water and copper and iron, together, could produce electricity.

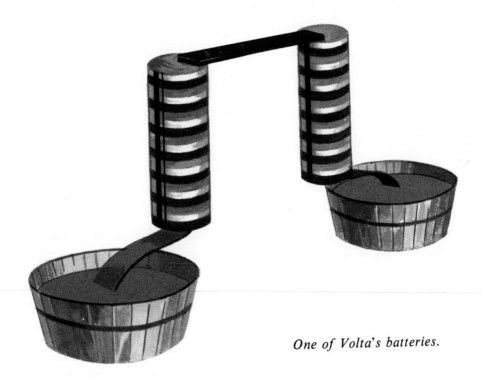

One of Volta's batteries.

No matter how many times Volta touched the pile, it always gave him a shock. And if he kept his hands on the pile, electricity flowed through his body in a steady stream, or current. His pile of metal sheets, in other words, produced electricity continuously, and by chemical means.

Volta had invented the *battery*, the device men needed in order to make the first practical use of electrical energy. (A unit of electrical measurement called the volt is named in his honor.)

Electricity and Atoms

SCIENTISTS STILL CAN'T ANSWER all the questions that are asked about electricity. But they have worked out a theory to explain what happens when electricity is produced.

Electricity is produced, according to this theory, because a change takes place in the number of electrons whirling around the nucleus of an atom.

Scientists believe that there are electrical charges of two kinds, called positive and negative, in each atom. They believe that the protons inside the atom's nucleus are charged with *positive electricity*, and that the whirling electrons are charged with *negative electricity*.

There is an old saying, "Opposites attract each other, and likes repel each other." This seems to be true in the case of positive protons and negative electrons.

You can upset the balance of the atoms in your hair.

Protons repel protons. Electrons repel electrons. But protons and electrons attract each other.

An atom is usually in balance electrically. This means that the amount of negative charge in the electrons is usually equal to the amount of positive charge in the protons inside the nucleus. And atoms that are in balance neither repel nor attract each other. But this balance may be upset by moving away some of the electrons from an atom.

You can upset the balance of the atoms in your hair by a simple experiment. The experiment works best on a dry day.

Comb your hair briskly for several minutes, and then put the comb down. You will notice that your hair stands up, as if each hair were trying to move away from the rest. Now pick up the comb again and hold it close to your head. Your hair will bend outward as if trying to touch it. You may hear a faint crackling sound. If it is dark you may see tiny sparks.

This is what happened during the experiment:

The comb, striking the atoms in your hair, carried off some of the whirling electrons. This put the atoms out of balance, because they now had fewer negative electrons than positive protons. The atoms thus became positively charged. And since positively charged atoms try to repel each other, the atoms in your hair tried to move away from each other. This made your hair stand straight up, as each hair tried to move away from the rest.

The atoms in your comb collected those extra negative electrons. Therefore the atoms in the comb became negatively charged. So, when you brought the negative comb near the positive hair, the two attracted each other. The extra electrons leaped back to the hair, restoring the electrical balance of the atoms. Those leaping electrons made that small crackling sound, and created those tiny sparks.

Static Electricity and Current Electricity

THE KIND OF ELECTRICITY that can be stored on a comb, or in a Leyden jar, is called *static electricity*. Static, which means "not active," or "not moving," describes this sort of electricity very well.

Current electricity is electricity that has a continuous flow, like the flow of a current of water. It is a continuous movement of electrons.

In a battery like the one Volta made, the chemical action of the salt water has the effect of taking electrons from the copper and putting them onto the iron. When the iron sheets can't hold any more electrons, the shifting stops. The iron is then negatively charged, because it has too many electrons. The copper is positively charged because it doesn't have enough electrons.

When Volta put one hand on the first iron sheet in his pile, and the other on the last copper sheet, his body became a sort of bridge between the two. Instantly the extra electrons on the iron moved across that bridge and back to the copper. The shock Volta felt was the movement of electrons through his body to restore the positive-negative balance of the battery.

If Volta had connected the two ends of his battery with a copper wire, the electrons would have had a much better bridge to cross. This is because electrons can move more easily through copper than through a human body. A scientist would say that copper is a better *conductor* than the body is.

Copper and certain other metals are particularly good electrical conductors because their electrons are easily jolted out of place. Only a material which has easily movable electrons is a good conductor. Any material with tightly held electrons will not conduct electricity and is called an *insulator*. Rubber, glass, and porcelain are good insulators.

Men quickly found uses for the new source of energy that they had discovered. The first telegraph machines and the first telephones were operated by batteries. But batteries were expensive and soon wore out. Their metal sheets, which scientists call *electrodes*, simply crumbled away. They were eaten up by the chemical action. So people began to seek a better and cheaper method of producing electric current.

The clue to that method came from a magnetic compass in the laboratory of a Danish scientist. But since a magnetic compass is simply a magnet free to swing about, it would be more accurate to say that the clue was really a magnet.

Magnets and Electricity

Today most people know about the qualities of magnets. They know that one end of a needle-like sliver of magnetized iron always points to the north when the needle is free to spin around at the end of a thread or on a pin run through its center. The end that points north is called its *north pole*. The opposite end is called its *south pole*.

The north poles of two magnets repel each other. The south poles of two magnets repel each other. But the north pole of one magnet attracts the south pole of

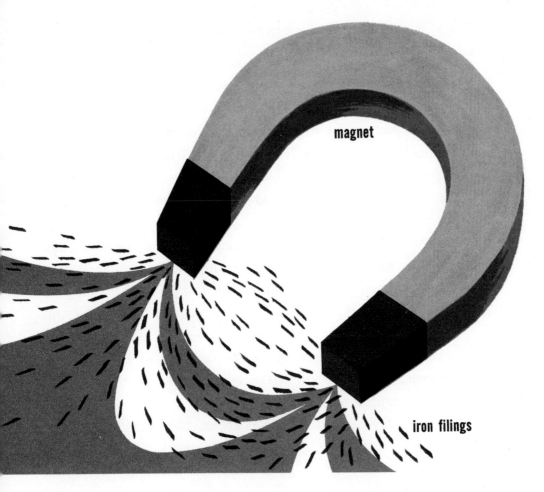

The area of magnetic force around a magnet is called the magnetic field.

another magnet. And one magnet does not have to be right beside another magnet in order to attract or repel it. Magnets can exert their force at a distance. The area of magnetic force around a magnet is called the *magnetic field*. Within this field are the magnet's invisible *lines of force*, which extend from one pole to the other.

Dr. Hans Oersted's compass was lying on his desk one day in 1820 when the event occurred that made electrical history. He was demonstrating to his students a Volta battery to which copper wires had been attached. Suddenly one of the wires slipped from his hand and happened to fall very close to the compass. Instantly the compass needle shifted from its usual north-south position.

The Danish professor was amazed and puzzled. His compass needle had behaved in the way it would behave if the compass had been affected by another magnet. But Oersted didn't see how the wire could affect his compass in that way. He picked the wire up. The compass needle returned to its usual position. He put the wire near the compass again—and once more the needle changed position.

Oersted wrote an article about the needle's strange behavior. It stirred up a lot of curiosity, and set scientists to performing experiments that resulted in several important discoveries.

The first was made in France by André Ampère. (His name was later given to a unit of electrical measurement called an *ampere*.) He discovered that a wire becomes a magnet whenever electricity is flowing through it. Ampère had explained the behavior of Oersted's compass. Its magnetized needle had been affected by the magnetized wire attached to the Volta battery.

Another French scientist put a needle inside a small

coil of wire and sent an electric current through the wire. The needle immediately became strongly magnetized. He had discovered how to make what we call an *electro-magnet*.

The next important step was taken in England by Michael Faraday, a blacksmith's son. Faraday was born at a time when poor children received very little education, and his family was very poor. At the age of fourteen he became apprenticed to a bookbinder.

Although he had to work from dawn to dark, he still found time to read many of the books brought to his master for binding. The books on science interested him most of all.

One day a customer happened to hear Faraday discuss some of the scientific subjects he had read about. The customer was amazed by all that Faraday had taught himself. He invited the young man to a series of lectures by a famous chemist, Sir Humphrey Davy. Faraday listened spellbound to everything Davy said, and afterward sent him a neat copy of the notes he had made at the lectures. The great scientist was also impressed with the young man's intelligent interest in chemistry. Soon Davy found young Faraday a job washing bottles in the laboratory of the great Royal Institution.

Faraday was delighted to be in a laboratory. He learned how to hurry through his dull tasks so that he could attempt a few experiments on his own. By the time he was twenty-five, people were beginning to hear

Faraday with one of the first machines to produce electricity from mechanical motion.

of the work of this brilliant young scientist. Less than ten years later the blacksmith's son was the director of the Royal Institution laboratory, and on the road to world fame.

By then Faraday had done a great deal of thinking about electricity and magnetism. He knew that Ampère had shown that electricity can produce magnetism. Faraday wondered if perhaps the opposite might also be true—that magnetism could produce electricity. The idea seemed far-fetched to most men. But Faraday performed an experiment that proved his guess to be correct.

First he connected a coil of wire to a galvanometer. This instrument (named after the Dr. Galvani who experimented with frog legs) can detect the presence of even very small quantities of electricity. Then Faraday pushed one end of a straight bar magnet into the center of the wire coil. The galvanometer reacted instantly. It showed that a surge of electricity had flowed through the wire when the magnet was moving into the coil. When Faraday pulled the magnet out of the coil, the galvanometer showed that another surge of electricity had flowed through the wire.

As long as the magnet was stationary inside the coil, no electricity flowed in the wire. But when the magnet was moving, either into the coil or out of it, there was electricity flowing in the wire.

It made no difference, Faraday discovered, whether he moved the magnet into the coil, or moved the coil over the magnet. As long as the coil of wire was crossing the magnet's lines of force, an electric current was moving in the wire.

Faraday had discovered how to transform mechanical energy into electrical energy by means of magnetism. He made it possible for us to build the devices we call *electric generators*. With these generators we transform the mechanical energy of huge steam and water turbines into the electrical energy we use. Without electric generators we could not produce the vast amounts of electricity the world needs today.

Michael Faraday is sometimes called the father of electricity because of his important discovery. (An electrical unit of measurement, the farad, is named in his honor.)

Electric Motors

ALMOST FORTY YEARS WENT BY, after Faraday's important discovery, before successful generators could be manufactured. Scientists first had to learn a great deal more about electricity than anyone knew in 1831. While they were experimenting with coils of wires and magnets, they were also learning how to make electric motors.

An *electric motor* is a device that changes electrical energy into motion. A typical electric motor consists of three main parts:

1. A stationary case lined with electro-magnets.
2. A shaft which revolves inside the case when the motor is operating.
3. Electro-magnets attached to the shaft.

When electricity enters the motor, the current flows through all the electro-magnets. The south pole of every magnet on the shaft tries to move toward the nearest north pole of the stationary magnets inside the case. And the north pole of every shaft magnet tries to move toward the nearest stationary south pole. This magnetic pull makes the shaft turn.

Of course the shaft would stop turning as soon as all the opposing magnetic poles were facing each other. But this never happens, because an electric motor contains a device called a *commutator*. The commutator constantly changes the direction of the current flowing through the coils of the shaft magnets. And this change of current direction changes the magnetic poles from north to south and from south to north. Each time the shaft magnetic poles are about to match up with the stationary magnetic poles, this change takes place. The commutator reverses the poles of the shaft magnets, and the magnetic pull continues.

An electric motor changes electrical energy into motion.

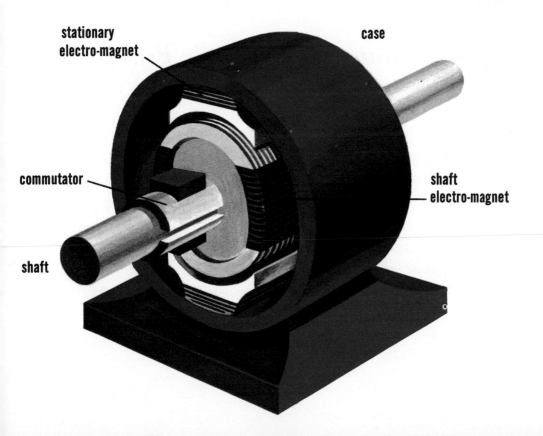

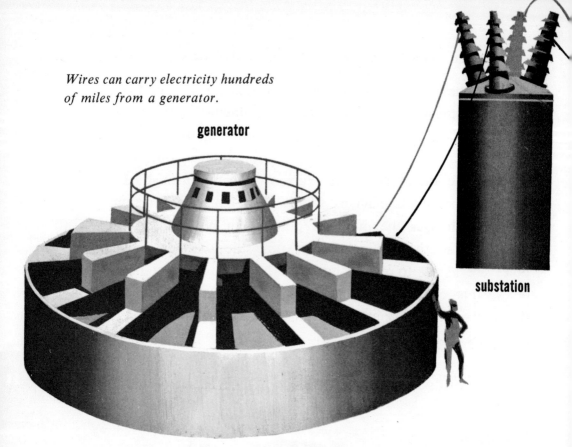

Wires can carry electricity hundreds of miles from a generator.

generator

substation

The Advantages of Electric Power

For many purposes electricity is the most useful form of energy we have.

Electricity can supply almost any amount of quiet and easily controlled power to operate all sorts of machines. Electric motors can be made large enough to propel ocean liners, or small enough to fit into a thimble to operate scientific equipment.

Electricity can warm a cup of milk or melt the toughest metals.

Electricity can extract oxygen and hydrogen from

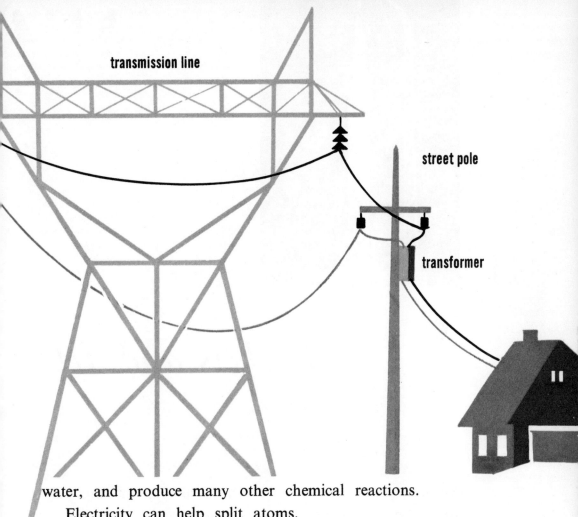

transmission line

street pole

transformer

water, and produce many other chemical reactions.

Electricity can help split atoms.

Electricity powers electronic devices as simple as a heat regulator in our home, and as complicated as the remote control of an orbiting satellite.

Electricity can be produced in one place and used in another. It can be generated where there is plenty of cheap water power to spin generators, and sent hundreds of miles silently over wires to be used in a distant city.

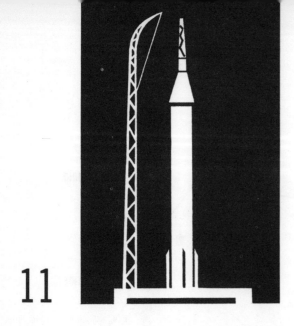

11

Rockets and Jets

MODERN ROCKETS AND JETS—from the tiniest fireworks rocket to the biggest jet-plane engine or rocket missile—all operate on the same principle. It is called the principle or law of *reaction*. Its name explains why rockets and jets are called *reaction engines*.

The law of reaction states: For every action there is an equal and opposite reaction.

A good example is a hunter firing a gun. In this case the *action* is the forward zoom of the bullet. The "equal and opposite" *reaction* is the backward kick of the gun against the hunter's shoulder.

Another good example is a swimmer diving from the side of an unanchored rowboat. The swimmer is usually surprised, when he comes up, to see how far the boat has moved from its original position. The boat has reacted to the swimmer's act of diving. And the movement of the boat is always in the opposite direction from that of the dive that caused it.

If a long parade of swimmers could dive from a single boat, one after the other, the boat would move steadily in the direction opposite to the divers.

This is just about what happens in a reaction engine. The "divers" are molecules of hot gases shooting out of the engine's nozzle. Of course a single molecule of gas is so tiny that it has very little push. But the action of billions of molecules, shooting out of a nozzle at terrific speed, can produce a powerful reaction. It can lift huge planes into the air, or send rockets far out into space.

The hot gases required by every reaction engine are obtained by burning a mixture of fuel and oxygen.

As a diver moves from a boat, the boat moves the other way.

Since this mixture is burned inside the engine, a reaction engine is really another member of the family of internal-combustion engines. Therefore the designer of a reaction engine must devise a method for bringing oxygen into his engine where it can be mixed with the fuel.

This problem has been solved in several different ways. One way produced the *rocket*. A second way produced the *ramjet*. A third way produced the *turbojet*.

Rockets

A MODERN MILITARY or scientific rocket is a tremendously complicated machine, with thousands of mechanical and electrical parts. But a rocket does not have to be complicated in order to work.

A small fireworks rocket is simply a fuel-packed cardboard tube, closed at one end and open at the other. The closed end may be covered by a pointed cap. The open end may have a stick attached to it. The stick holds the rocket upright while it is being set off. Like the tail of a kite, the stick also helps keep the flying object on its course.

The fuel packed inside the fireworks rocket's tube is a small charge of gunpowder. Gunpowder, like other explosives such as TNT and dynamite, is made up of several chemicals. Some burn so swiftly that, under certain conditions, they explode. Others, when heated, supply the oxygen necessary for the burning. They give the rocket a built-in oxygen supply.

The powder in a rocket isn't supposed to explode, of course. An explosion would blow the rocket to bits instead of sending it up into the air. But the combustion inside the rocket must take place so rapidly that it is just short of an explosion.

This rapid combustion produces so much hot gas in the tube that the gas spurts out through the rear opening in a powerful burst, or exhaust jet. The reaction to that rearward-moving jet sends the rocket zooming forward.

When the powder in a rocket is pressed into a solid cake, the rocket is called a *solid-fuel rocket*. Some of our big modern rockets belong to this group.

Other modern rockets use a liquid fuel. The first liquid-fuel rocket ever made was launched in Massachusetts on March 16, 1926. The man who built it and set it off was a quiet, shy physics professor, Dr. Robert Hutchings Goddard.

Goddard spent most of his life working on rockets. He first began to experiment with them in 1914. Then the only rockets most people knew about were fireworks rockets. In 1920, when Goddard said that a three-stage rocket could reach the moon, practically everyone laughed at him. When he began to launch his liquid-fuel rockets, the police made him stop. They said his experiments were noisy and dangerous.

But Goddard was a determined man. He left Massachusetts and set up a rocket-launching site in New Mexico. There he and a few assistants went on building rockets. Each one taught Goddard more about the science of rocketry. He learned how to steer a rocket. He learned how to cool a rocket motor so that it would not burn up in its own tremendous heat. The men who build today's giant rockets owe a great deal to this quiet New Englander.

Scientists are now working toward a nuclear rocket engine that would be different from both solid- and liquid-fuel engines. In this engine the fuel, hydrogen, would not burn with oxygen to provide the exhaust jet. Instead the hydrogen would be forced through the great heat of a nuclear reactor. There the hydrogen would expand tremendously and hydrogen molecules would be shot out of the engine in a powerful jet.

Goddard launched the first liquid-fuel rocket in 1926.

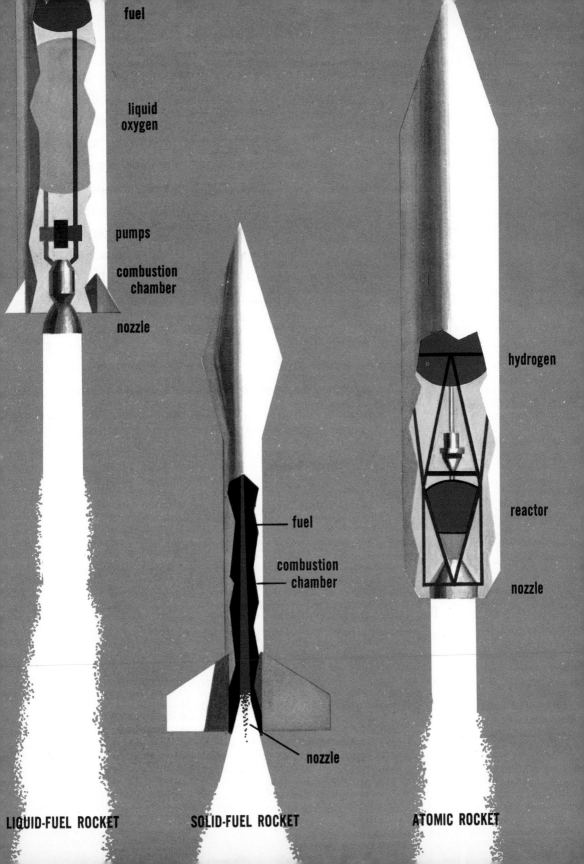

fuel

liquid
oxygen

pumps

combustion
chamber

nozzle

fuel

combustion
chamber

nozzle

hydrogen

reactor

nozzle

LIQUID-FUEL ROCKET   **SOLID-FUEL ROCKET**   **ATOMIC ROCKET**

Another experimental rocket engine works by shooting out a stream of electrically charged atoms, instead of the gas molecules shot out by ordinary rocket engines. A charged atom is called an ion. So this engine is called an *ion engine*. The ions in these engines are speeded up by electrical means to a tremendous velocity before being ejected. The exhaust jets of some ion engines have reached speeds of 100,000 miles per hour.

Ion engines have very little thrust or push. They are designed to be used after a vehicle has reached outer space. There, where there is no air resistance or gravitational pull to fight against, even a tiny ion engine could propel a space vehicle.

Every rocket engine carries within itself all that is necessary to form an exhaust jet. In this one way, rocket engines are different from other kinds of reaction engines.

The Ramjet

THE RAMJET REACTION ENGINE obtains its oxygen from the air. So a ramjet cannot operate in outer space, which is airless.

The ramjet consists of a tube, open at both ends, containing a fuel supply, a combustion chamber, and various controlling and regulating devices.

As a ramjet zooms forward through the atmosphere, air is driven into the tube through its open front end.

Engineers say the air is *rammed* in. Their phrase gave this engine its name.

The great rush of incoming air is compressed inside the combustion chamber. There a spray of fuel is mixed with the compressed air, and the mixture is burned. The flaming gases given off by the combustion jet out through the rear of the engine. Thus—by the law of reaction—they drive the engine forward.

The ramjet is a good and simple engine. It has only one serious drawback. Unless it is moving at high speed —about 300 miles per hour—not enough air is rammed into the tube to maintain its combustion. This means that a plane using a ramjet engine must be launched by some device which will give it the speed it needs to start its engine. But launching devices are expensive

The ramjet, though a good and simple engine, requires separate launching equipment.

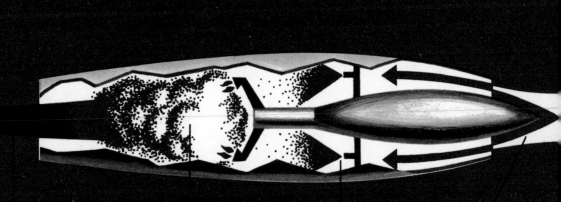

exhaust jet   combustion   fuel spray   air intake
                      chamber

and complicated. That is why ramjets are seldom used except in experimental work.

The Turbojet

THE TURBOJET ENGINE is very much like a gas turbine. It has a shaft that runs the length of the engine, with an air compressor at the front and a turbine at the rear. The air compressor forces air into the combustion chamber, where it is mixed with fuel and burned. This combustion produces hot gases that spurt out rearward, spinning the turbine and forming the jet.

The only real difference between a turbojet and a gas turbine is in the way these two engines use the power of the flaming gases.

In the case of the gas turbine, most of the power of the hot gases is used to turn the turbine. This is because the purpose of a gas turbine is to provide rotating power to turn a propeller. A turbojet, on the other hand, isn't meant to turn anything. So designers of turbojet engines generally try to use as much of the engine's power as possible for producing a powerful jet.

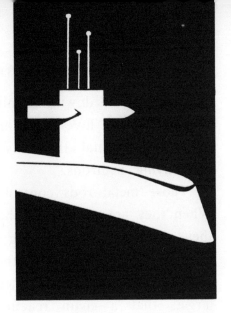

12

Nuclear Reactors

WHEN AN ATOMIC CHAIN reaction is properly controlled, the rate of atom-splitting is slowed down. The result is a steady supply of heat energy which can be harnessed to do useful work.

The device that controls the rate of atom-splitting is called a *nuclear reactor*. It has thick massive walls, made of metal or concrete or both. The reactor's interior is honeycombed with holes so that it looks something like a gigantic block of Swiss cheese. Into some of these holes are fitted long metal tubes called *canisters*. The canisters are filled with uranium or some other fissionable material. Other holes contain rods made of cadmium or some other metal that has the ability to absorb and hold flying neutrons.

Those metal rods control the speed of atom-splitting. When they are pushed all the way down into their holes, they absorb so many flying neutrons that a chain reaction cannot get started. If the control rods were removed entirely, so many flying neutrons would strike nuclear targets that a chain reaction would take place in an instant, and there would be an explosion. But the control rods can be pulled part way out of the holes. They can be regulated so that the number of neutrons striking nuclear targets is just enough to keep a chain reaction going at a safe, steady rate.

The heat produced in a nuclear reactor must first be taken out of the reactor before it can be put to work. This is done by circulating various substances—such as gases or water—through pipes that lead through the reactor to a boiler. Those substances absorb heat inside the reactor, and then transfer that heat to the water in the boiler. When the water boils, it is transformed into high-pressure steam that can drive turbines. Those turbines, in turn, may operate an electric generator.

A single pound of fissionable uranium can produce about as much energy as 3,000,000 pounds of coal. This suggests that it might be much cheaper to produce electricity by using atomic heat than by burning coal or

Heat from a nuclear reactor may be used to power a steam turbine. The turbine may, in turn, operate an electric generator.

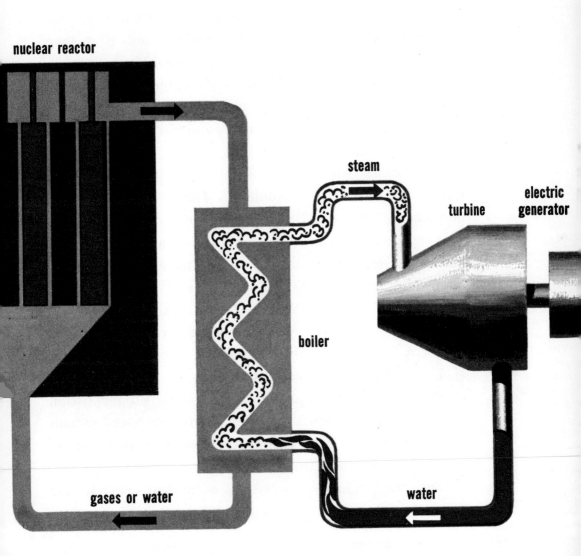

nuclear reactor

steam

electric
generator

turbine

boiler

gases or water

water

fuel oil. But, for the present at least, atomic heat is more expensive to produce than heat from oil or coal. One reason is that nuclear reactors cost a great deal to build. Another is that their fuel is very expensive.

The uranium most often used for a reactor's fuel is uranium-235. Separating this kind of uranium from the two other kinds also found in uranium ore is a long process. And there is very little uranium-235 in uranium ore. It is necessary to refine 2,000 pounds of ore in order to obtain about 20 pounds of fissionable material. This refining process, and the scarcity of uranium-235, lead to its high cost.

Two other substances can also be used as reactor fuels—thorium and plutonium. They are made by bombarding uranium-238 with neutrons of uranium-235. This process is also more expensive than pumping oil out of the ground or digging coal. Engineers are working constantly to bring these costs down. And they are having some success. Within a few years, experts say, nuclear-fission reactors will supply energy for generating electricity at a reasonable cost.

Even if reactor fuels were cheap, however, there would still be serious drawbacks to using atomic fission for producing power. Atomic fission releases radiant energy as well as heat energy—and some of that radiant energy is dangerous to life.

The thick massive walls of a nuclear reactor are designed to prevent the escape of dangerous radiation.

Nuclear reactors power some large submarines.

Thinner and lighter walls would not be safe. That is why every reactor must have a certain bulk and weight.

On land it is possible to build a thick-walled reactor to operate a huge power station. It is possible to build a reactor small enough to put aboard a surface ship or a large submarine. But the smallest nuclear plant that can be built today would be too heavy and bulky for an airplane, a truck, or a car. So, for the present at least, the energy of nuclear fission is being used only in large land power stations and aboard large ships.

There is another method of obtaining energy from atoms that may some day provide the world with cheap, abundant, safe power. This method joins or fuses atoms together. It is called *atomic fusion.*

Atomic Fusion

IN ATOMIC FUSION the nucleus of one atom is joined to the nucleus of another. This fusion produces an entirely different atom. During the process of fusion, some of the matter in the original atoms is changed into energy (just as some matter is changed into energy in atomic fission).

The amount of energy produced by atomic fusion is many times greater than the energy produced by splitting atoms. The tremendous energy of the sun is believed to result from atomic fusion—from the fusion of hydrogen atoms to form the quite different atoms of helium.

Atomic fusion takes place only under great heat. The fusion of hydrogen atoms in the sun takes place because of its terrifically high internal temperature— about 35,000,000 degrees Fahrenheit. Nothing on earth can ever be heated to that high temperature. But the explosion of an atomic bomb creates a temperature of 2,000,000 degrees. That is why scientists decided that it might be possible to fuse hydrogen atoms in the heat of an atomic bomb. In 1952 they first attempted the experiment.

They put hydrogen in a container with an atomic bomb, and exploded it on a small uninhabited island in the South Pacific. The hydrogen atoms fused. They made a blast several hundred times more powerful than the atomic-bomb blast that provided the heat. It was the biggest man-made explosion ever produced. The energy produced by that hydrogen bomb, as it was called, completely destroyed the island.

Scientists know there would be many advantages in atomic fusion as a source of energy. They know that the heat of fusion is what they call "clean heat." They mean that it does not produce any dangerous radioactive waste.

They also know how to obtain all the fuel they could ever want for atomic fusion. That fuel, *heavy hydrogen*, is obtained from *heavy water*. And since there is a little bit of heavy water in every drop of ordinary water, the world's oceans hold an almost unlimited supply of this fuel.

But no one has yet solved the basic problem of how to start hydrogen-atom fusion without using an atomic bomb as a "match" to set it off. This means that we are still far from being able to produce a controlled fusion chain reaction that could be used as a steady, safe source of energy.

One of the many problems that remain to be solved arises from the fact that every known substance would vaporize under the heat of hydrogen fusion. Therefore no known substance could be used successfully as a container for fusing atoms.

This particular problem may be solved because of a change that takes place in a gas when it is heated to a high temperature. Then some of the atoms of the gas gain an electron, and some lose an electron. Those atoms are unbalanced electrically. Scientists describe them as being "charged with electricity."

Charged atoms can be controlled by magnetism. They can be slowed down or speeded up by a magnetic field. They can also be caged by a magnetic field—confined in a "corral" made of invisible magnetic lines of force. That is why scientists hope they will be able to build a container for nuclear fusion out of lines of force from tremendously powerful electro-magnets.

Inside this "magnetic bottle," hydrogen atoms could fuse and release their energy without coming in contact with any substance that would turn to vapor under high heat. This magnetic bottle might also help to start fusion, by squeezing the hydrogen atoms together and thus heating them.

Controlled fusion reaction, if it becomes possible, will probably generate electricity without the need for steam boilers, turbines, and electric generators. The reason for this goes back to Faraday's discovery: When a coil of copper wire, or any other conducting material, is passed through a magnetic field, an electric current is generated in the coil.

High-temperature hydrogen is a conductor of electricity because it contains charged atoms. Therefore an electric current would be generated inside a "magnetic bottle." This means that the heat energy of hydrogen would be converted directly into electrical energy.

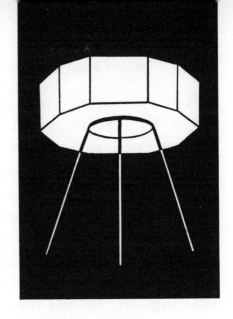

Power for the Future

EVEN IF THE ENERGY of nuclear fusion and fission some-day proves to be the world's most important source of power, it seems likely that other power sources will still be needed for certain purposes. Non-atomic power will probably go on being useful for automobiles. Non-atomic power will probably go on providing electricity in small remote villages where large-scale atomic-energy power plants would not be practical.

Probably mankind will continue to use the same fossil fuels—coal, natural gas, and petroleum—which provide us with so much of the power we use today. But if we continue to burn those fuels as fast as we do now, we will use them up. That is why scientists are interested in developing new and more efficient methods of producing power from those fuels. Greater efficiency will make our fuel supply last longer.

The scientists who are trying to produce more and more power for the world's ever-growing populations are working along two lines at once. Some are developing safe ways to use our new atomic sources of power. Others are trying to improve our current methods for using older and more familiar power sources.

In most cases those scientists are working toward the production of more electricity—that form of energy that has proved its special usefulness to mankind. Some of the methods they have been working on combine new ideas with very old ones.

Electricity can be produced from many other forms of energy: water power, wind power, heat, chemical energy, atomic energy, and light. Each of those sources, even man's early servants, water and wind power, will be used to produce power in the future.

Water Power and Wind Power

EXPERTS BELIEVE that the twice-daily flow of the tide, in some coastal areas where the tides run very high, could be put to work. The water could be trapped, detoured through turbines on its way back to the sea, and thus made to produce electricity.

Tidal power is not steady power. There would be periods each day when those turbines would not turn. It would be necessary to have a steam or Diesel or nuclear generating plant to take over the job of producing electricity when the tidal generators were still. But during the hours when the tides were running, those fuel-using generators could stand idle. Thus large amounts of expensive fuel would be saved.

There are many rivers in the world whose power could be tapped in the future. One small Central American country, Guatemala, has fifty times as much water power as it is now using. In Africa, Kenya has enough streams and rivers to produce more than 5,000,000 horsepower. In such lands more and more power will be needed as the countries become industrialized, and the use of water power will certainly be increased there.

No one expects that wind power will ever produce vast quantities of electricity, since winds do not blow steadily enough in most parts of the world. But in an area of fairly steady winds, a windmill could generate enough electricity to provide lights for a small village.

In other areas, with less dependable winds, a windmill might still be useful. It could turn a generator whenever a wind was blowing. That same generator could be operated by a Diesel engine, say, when the wind failed.

Engineers also hope to make better use of wind power by designing efficient windmills that would operate even in very gentle breezes.

More Electricity From Heat Energy

WHENEVER ENERGY IS CHANGED from one form to another, some of it is wasted. When petroleum is burned, its chemical energy is transformed into heat, and the heat in turn is transformed into electricity. In this roundabout method, less than half the energy of the fuel becomes electricity. The rest is wasted.

This is why scientists have been working to develop less wasteful methods for producing electricity directly from heat. So far they have not been completely successful. Some of the methods they have developed are very expensive. None of them has yet produced electricity in large amounts. But all these methods are still in the experimental stage, and scientists hope they will prove really useful in the future.

One method of transforming heat directly into electrical energy is called *thermoelectricity*—a name that simply means "heat electricity." Two different metals are put together in a tight joint, the joint is heated, and the heat sets an electric current flowing through the metals.

One early thermoelectric generator could produce only one watt—not enough power to light a tiny electric bulb. Further experiments, using different metals and higher temperatures, made it possible to produce 100 watts of electricity from a small gas flame. Today much larger thermoelectric generators are being built.

The thermoelectric generator is still very inefficient. The best one made, so far, wastes seven-eighths of the heat it uses. But one such generator, heated by radioactive waste material from nuclear-fission reactors, has already found use in a satellite orbiting the earth.

The atoms in the generator's radioactive waste split and release energy without any outside help, just as the atoms of radium do. But their rate of splitting is much greater than that of radium. It goes on fast enough to generate about five watts of electricity—and this is enough to operate a satellite's radio transmitter.

The radioactive "furnace" of this generator "wears out" eventually. But it lasts long enough to supply as much electricity as could be obtained from more than a thousand pounds of ordinary chemical batteries. The little thermoelectric generator weighs only five pounds. That is why it has proved valuable in spite of its inefficiency.

This type of thermoelectric generator—sometimes called a nuclear battery—is also being used to power scientific instruments in the Arctic, and deep down in the ocean. Those instruments are used to collect the information scientists need in their studies of weather and of the ocean's depths. And that information is sent back to a base by radio transmitters also operated by the thermoelectric generator. Such thermoelectric-powered installations are expected to operate on their own for years.

Experiments with the joining of two different metals have also led to devices that may save fuels in another way. If a current from a battery or a generator is passed in one direction through a joint of two metals, the joint becomes hot. If the current is made to flow in the opposite direction, the joint grows cold. Some manufacturers are already making refrigerators that are cooled by this method. Other manufacturers are building experimental heaters using the same method.

In the future, perhaps, houses will have thermoelectric units built into their walls. Pressing one switch will cause them to heat the house. Pressing another switch will cause them to cool it.

A second kind of electric generator using heat and metal is called a *thermionic converter*. It consists of two metal plates in a vacuum. One plate is called the *emitter*. The other is called the *collector*. When the emitter is heated to a high temperature, about 4,000 degrees Fahrenheit, it gives off, or emits, electrons. These emitted electrons move to the collector plate, much as extra electrons moved to one of the electrodes in Volta's battery. And, just as in a battery, these electrons will flow through a wire and form an electric current.

Thermionic converters in use now produce only very small quantities of electricity. And they produce it very inefficiently. But they are being constantly improved. In one new type, the metal plates are surrounded by a certain gas instead of being in a vacuum. This speeds up the rate at which the electrons are emitted. Another experimental thermionic converter, which needs only 2,000 degrees of heat, could be operated by concentrated rays of the sun and used to supply electricity for satellites in space. Still another, made to fit inside a fuel canister of a nuclear reactor, converts some of the great nuclear heat directly into electricity.

A thermionic converter, heated by the exhaust jet of a rocket, has supplied electricity for guiding the rocket.

Michael Faraday's discovery that magnetism could produce electricity has been used in the development of a third new kind of generator. This one also produces electricity directly from heat energy. Usually this device is called an *MHD generator*, because its full name is so long: *magnetohydrodynamic generator*.

Faraday produced electricity, you remember, by passing a conductor of electricity through the lines of force of a magnet. Faraday used a coil of copper wire as his conductor. There is no coil of wire in an MHD generator. Instead there is a stream of gas heated until its atoms become electrically charged, and therefore able to conduct electricity.

The hot gas is pumped through a ceramic tube past the poles of powerful electro-magnets. As the gas passes through the magnetic lines of force, a flow of electrons is started in it just as in the copper coils of an ordinary generator. This flow of electrons is a current of electricity.

The MHD generator, which can be heated either by an oil-oxygen furnace or by a nuclear reactor, is still in the experimental stage. But experts believe that they can improve it to the point where it will be as efficient as rotating electric generators in use today.

A fourth new method for obtaining electricity from heat energy makes use of the limitless supply of free heat from the molten core of the earth. This kind of heat is called *geothermal*, which means "earth-heat." Geothermal power keeps Yellowstone National Park's famous geysers erupting year after year.

In some parts of the world geothermal heat has already been put to practical use. The 50,000 inhabitants of Reykjavik, capital of Iceland, warm houses and greenhouses with heat from Iceland's steam and hot-water wells.

The geysers and boiling springs of North Island, New Zealand, operate a huge geothermal-electric plant there.

Steam from hot-water wells near Florence, Italy, piped to huge turbines, generates tremendous quantities

Geothermal-electric plant in New Zealand.

of electricity. Enough electric energy is produced there to run all of Italy's railroad trains.

Geothermal power, many experts believe, could be tapped in other parts of the world too. They think it is available even in places where it does not make itself visible in the form of geysers and boiling springs. That is why geologists, geophysicists, and geochemists have now joined in the great search for more power for the future. They are seeking new sources of geothermal power, which may some day replace some of the power now obtained from our dwindling supply of fossil fuels.

More Electricity From Chemical Energy

ANOTHER ELECTRIC GENERATOR for which experimenters have great hopes is called the *fuel cell*.

A fuel cell has two electrodes, similar to those in an ordinary battery. But it does not wear out, as an ordinary battery does.

The chemical energy it uses comes from some chemical fuel, such as hydrogen. Inside the fuel cell this fuel is combined with oxygen. As it combines, some of its chemical energy is converted into an electric current. The fuel cell will go on producing electricity as long as it is fed with oxygen and the chemical fuel.

Today the fuel cell is not very efficient. But scientists believe that it may someday be developed to the point where it can convert more than four-fifths of its fuel energy into electrical energy. In that case the fuel cell would be about twice as efficient as the most efficient steam or Diesel-driven generator now in use.

Highly efficient fuel cells might someday replace the huge steam-turbine generating plants which produce so much of the electricity used today. They might also replace many of the gasoline and Diesel engines now used for transportation. Since they have no moving parts and operate silently, fuel cells might provide electricity for electric motors that would drive automobiles noiselessly over our highways.

Even today an inefficient fuel cell has some advantages over other sources of electricity. A 30-pound fuel cell can supply as much electricity as an engine-driven generator weighing twice as much, or batteries weighing almost three times as much. And a man can carry a 30-pound fuel cell on his back, pack fashion. This is why military men are already planning to use fuel cells to supply silent power for portable radio and radar equipment.

Another recent development along these lines is called the *bio battery*, from the Greek word *bios*, which means life. Inside this new battery there are living bacteria. The bacteria give off chemicals which can transform many cheap, common substances into fuels for the battery. Sugar, potatoes, and even sea water may some day produce electricity from bio batteries, with the help of these invisible microbes.

Making More Use of the Sun

WE HAVE ALREADY SEEN that the radiant energy of the sun can be converted into electricity by thermionic converters. Still another type of generator which scientists have developed also produces electricity from the sun's energy. This is the *solar cell* or *solar battery*.

A solar battery consists of many small thin sheets of a substance called silicon. When silicon is struck by light, electrons are pulled away from some of its atoms. These electrons form a current of electricity.

At present the solar battery, like most other new electric generators, is still inefficient. Only about one-seventh of the sunlight that strikes the silicon is converted into electrical energy. But the solar battery is useful for supplying power for satellites traveling in airless space, where the sunlight is much stronger than it is on earth.

Solar batteries can be used to charge ordinary storage batteries. This means that a storage battery and a solar battery, used together, can provide electricity for equipment that uses electric current every hour of the day and night.

A radio beacon could make good use of these two kinds of batteries. During the night the beacon would operate on electricity from its storage battery. Then, after sunrise, it would operate on its solar battery. The

In some satellites, hundreds of solar cells convert sunlight into electricity.

solar battery, at the same time, would be recharging the storage battery for its next period of service after sunset.

One very simple sun-using device is the solar cooker. It is already being used in India. A solar cooker is nothing more than a polished aluminum reflector, which focuses the sun's rays on a pot of food. This kind of "stove" will probably also prove useful in many of the hot desert regions of the world where fuel is scarce and expensive.

A similar but larger device is the solar furnace. One of these furnaces, built in France, consists of several hundred mirrors. These mirrors are fitted together to form one large round reflecting surface about 35 feet in diameter. This big reflector is mounted on a circular track, so that it can be turned to face the sun whenever the sun is shining. The enormous amount of sunlight which it catches is concentrated on a single small spot. At this spot the heat reaches temperatures higher than 5,000 degrees Fahrenheit.

This heat can be used to boil water to operate a steam turbine. Or the heat could be transformed more directly into electrical energy by means of one of the new thermoelectric generators.

Of course solar power—like wind power and tidal power—is not constant. To produce a steady supply of electricity, day and night, a solar furnace would have to be used along with some other type of generating plant.

A solar cooker focuses the sun's rays on a pot of food.

But an electric plant that now operates entirely on petroleum would burn much less fuel if a solar furnace provided the steam for its turbines part of the time.

A Job for Our Century

ABOUT 95 PER CENT of all the power used in the United States comes from fossil fuels. Petroleum alone supplies about 38 per cent of that power. Experts believe that, if we go on using up our petroleum supply at this rate, it will not last more than fifty years. Furthermore the population of the United States is growing so rapidly that it will naturally need more power in the future. And if the nation continues to obtain 38 per cent of its power from petroleum each year, the supply of that fuel will probably be used up even earlier.

The growing need for more power in the United States gives only a hint of the huge amounts of power that will be needed in other parts of the world. There are regions where industrialization is just beginning, where mechanical power is just starting to improve people's lives. There are other regions where muscles are still the only source of power. It is in those regions that people do not have enough food, hospitals, schools, and all the other things that are part of our modern civilization. It is in those regions that abundant mechanical power is most desperately needed.

These are the reasons why, today, so many scientists

and engineers are willing to spend their lives trying to develop new sources of power. They know that adding to the world's power supply is one of the most important jobs of this century.

Index

Betatron, 58
Bio battery, 131
"Bullet," atomic, 57, 58, 60

Cadmium rods, 114
Canisters, 113–14
Carburetor, 78
Chain reaction, 60–62
Chemical energy, 37, 46, 48
  electricity from, 130–131
Combustion chamber
  in gas turbine, 71
  in ramjet, 111
  in rocket, 109
  in turbojet, 112
Commutator, 101
Compass, magnetic, 94, 96
Compression stroke, 74, 80
Condensing tank, 28
Conductor, electrical, 93
Conservation of energy, 55
Conservation of matter, 55–56
Copper, as conductor, 93
Critical mass, 62
Curie, Marie, 52, 53
Curie, Pierre, 52–53
Current electricity, 93
Cycle of operation, 76
Cyclotron, 58
Cylinder
  in Diesel engine, 80–81

  in lift pump, 18–19
  in Newcomen engine, 24–25
  in Otto engine, 74–76
  in Somerset pump, 21–22
  in Watt engine, 28, 31

Daimler, Gottlieb, 78, 79
Davy, Humphrey, 97
Democritus, 50–51, 52
Diesel, Rudolph, 79, 80, 81
Diesel engine, 79–83
Double-acting steam engine, 31

Einstein, Albert, 55, 56
Electric generator, 99
Electric motor, 100, 102
Electrical energy, 37, 38, 84
Electricity
  battery for, 89–90
  from chemical energy, 130–31
  conductors of, 93
  current, 93
  from heat energy, 124–30
  increased production of, 122–36
  insulators for, 94
Electrodes, 94
Electro-magnets, 97, 100, 120
Electrons, 51, 52, 54, 84, 91
  in current electricity, 93
  negative charge of, 90, 92

The authors

SAM AND BERYL EPSTEIN have endeared themselves to hundreds of thousands of young readers through their more than seventy books. Over half of these have been information books in various fields, including science and biography.

For Random House they wrote ALL ABOUT PREHISTORIC CAVE MEN, after visiting prehistoric caves in France and Spain, and ALL ABOUT THE DESERT, which the New York *Herald Tribune Book Review* called "the best simple text on the subject we have seen."

As a lifelong tinkerer, Mr. Epstein has a special feeling for the subject matter of ALL ABOUT ENGINES AND POWER. In Southold, Long Island, N.Y., where he and his wife now live, power mowers and garden cultivators, outboard motors and electric pumps give him limitless opportunities to take mechanical contrivances apart to see what makes them run.

The artists

JOSEPH AND EVA CELLINI, who came to the United States following the Hungarian revolt of 1956, had been active in Budapest as artists and book illustrators. In this country they have specialized in the illustration of scientific and technical books. Mr. Cellini has also illustrated John Gunther's JULIUS CAESAR for the Landmark series. They share their New York City apartment with four cats and an indefinite number of kittens.

allabout
books

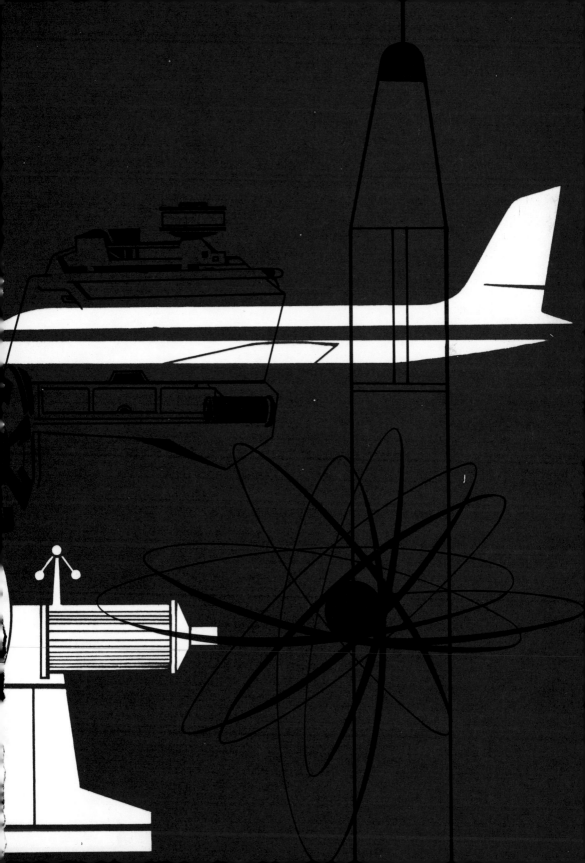